W9-BJL-594

THE BOBBSEY TWINS'

VISIT TO THE GREAT WEST

When Mrs. Bobbsey inherits the Half Circle Ranch in Santa Fe, New Mexico, the four Bobbsey twins, Nan, Bert, Freddie and Flossie, are delighted. Not only will it be thrilling to ride the range on the wiry little cow ponies, visit the Indian Reservation, and see the rodeo, but already there is a mystery to solve. The ranch foreman has reported that cattle are disappearing from the ranch, but so far there have been no clues to the rustlers.

There's another mystery, too. The Bobbseys' riding master in Lakeport, Mr. Hixon, tells them that his son Bud, who ran away ten years ago, may have gone out West. The twins are determined to find the young man and persuade him to return to his father.

How the Bobbseys accomplish their double purpose and what happens before the two mysteries are solved make a truly exciting story with an authentic background of the modern West.

THE BOBBSEY TWINS
By Laura Lee Hope

The frightened calf cleared the fence and kept on after
Freddie

The
Bobbsey Twins' Visit to the Great West

By

LAURA LEE HOPE

GROSSET & DUNLAP

Publishers   *New York*

© COPYRIGHT BY GROSSET & DUNLAP, INC., 1966
PUBLISHED SIMULTANEOUSLY IN CANADA
ALL RIGHTS RESERVED
ISBN: 0-448-08013-3

PRINTED IN THE UNITED STATES OF AMERICA
LIBRARY OF CONGRESS CATALOG CARD NO. AC66-10289
The Bobbsey Twins' Visit to the Great West

CONTENTS

THE BOBBSEY TWINS'
VISIT TO THE GREAT WEST

CHAPTER I

INDIANS!

"YOU heap big Injun chief!" said six-year-old Freddie Bobbsey to his brother Bert, who was twelve.

Bert wore fringed trousers and a feather headdress. He winked at his brown-eyed twin sister Nan, who was painting wide red streaks on his cheeks. "You be squaw," he said.

"Paint me, too, Nan!" begged Freddie. He and his twin, Flossie, both blond and blue-eyed, were the youngest members of the Bobbsey family. The four twins were playing with friends in the Bobbseys' back yard.

"Nellie will make you up," Nan replied.

"Will Daddy be home soon?" asked Flossie. "Mother won't tell us about the mystery we're going to solve out West till he comes. And I just can't wait!"

"I hope the mystery is about Indians and cowboys!" Freddie said, and gave a long-drawn-out war whoop by clapping one hand back and forth over his mouth. Then he ended with a *yippee-eye-aye*.

The other twins and their playmates laughed. Susie Larker and Teddy Blake were in the same grade as Freddie and Flossie. Nellie Parks and Charlie Mason were friends of the older twins.

"You Bobbseys sure are lucky," said Charlie, "being able to duck school and go on a trip."

"Yes we are," Nan agreed, "but did you hear what we have to do to make up the time?"

"No. What?"

"We have to study every day and each of us has to write a paper on Life and Customs on an Indian Reservation."

"So what?" said Freddie. "Come on! Let's play!"

All the children wore Indian headdresses. The boys had feathers around the band, but each of the girls had only one feather sticking up at the back. Charlie had insisted that this was the Indian custom.

"I want paint on my face!" Flossie cried.

"I don't think Indian girls ever put on war paint," Bert remarked.

"Well, I need something more than just this old feather to show I'm an Indian!" Flossie pouted a little. She looked in disgust at her brown shorts and yellow sweater.

"Me too!" piped up Susie Larker.

Nan had an idea. "There's an old Halloween costume upstairs," she said. "You and Susie can divide it."

She ran into the house and returned in a few minutes, her hands full. "Here you are," Nan said, tossing a brown fringed blouse and skirt to Flossie. "You can wear the top and Susie the skirt. And I brought all our play jewelry, too." She dumped a mass of many-colored necklaces and bracelets onto the picnic table.

"These are neat!" Nellie said. "We'll look like Indian princesses."

Flossie and Susie put on the blouse and skirt. Then the four girls hung the strings of beads around their necks and clasped bracelets on their arms.

"Aren't we bee-yoo-ti-ful?" Flossie cried.

Bert nodded, then said, "We ought to make tepees if we're going to have an Indian village."

"What's a tepee?" Flossie wanted to know.

"It's an Indian tent," Nan told her.

Bert went on, "I know where we can get the supports for it. Sam's working in the garage. I'll ask him if we can use those old Venetian blinds stored there."

"And I'll ask Dinah for some worn sheets!" Nan said, and ran toward the house again.

Dinah and Sam Johnson were a delightful colored couple who had lived with the Bobbseys for many years. Dinah helped Mrs. Bobbsey with the housework and Sam worked in the lumberyard owned by the twins' father.

Sam was washing the Bobbsey station wagon. He looked at Bert and grinned. "Great day!" he exclaimed. "I didn't know we had Injuns in Lakeport! I hope you didn't come to scalp me!"

Bert explained about the Indian village. Sam considered the problem, then picked up one of the blinds and began to remove the tapes.

"This ought to work fine," he remarked.

"Thanks, Sam," Bert said and hurried back to the yard with the bundle of slats.

In a few minutes Nan came from the house. "Dinah could give me only two sheets," she explained, "but we should be able to make a couple of tepees."

Freddie and Teddy held the slats steady, while Bert and Charlie pounded them into the ground, four for each tent. Then Nan and Nellie spread the sheets over the slats.

The children had just finished the job when two boys on bicycles rode into the yard. They were Danny Rugg and Jack Westley.

Danny and Jack were the same age as the older twins and Nellie and Charlie. They were not well liked because they played mean tricks.

"Hi, Danny! Hi, Jack!" said Bert.

"Hi!" Danny said. "Say, I've got a new archery set. I'll get it. Then Jack and I can play Indians with you."

"Okay," Bert said, but without enthusiasm.

The two boys pedaled off.

"Let's all take Indian names," Bert said. "I'll be Chief Roman Nose. Charlie can be White Antelope. Freddie, you're Little Wolf. Teddy, how about Red Cloud?"

"Suits me."

Nan named the girls. "I'm Singing Brook, and Flossie, how would you like to be Jumping Rabbit?"

"I love it." The little girl began to hop around the yard like a rabbit.

Nellie was Singing Dove and Susie became Little Crow. Each child dashed around pretending to be what his nickname indicated. The noise attracted the Bobbseys' dog Snap. The big shaggy white pet raced around with them barking loudly.

Flossie giggled. "You have to be an Indian dog." She stuck a feather in his collar.

Suddenly all the frivolity stopped. Danny and Jack had returned with the archery set. Bert propped the target against a tree. The target had three circles around the bull's-eye. An arrow could score 40, 30, or 20 points according to the circle in which it landed.

"Let's have two tribes," Charlie suggested. "Danny, you be a chief because it's your archery set. Bert, you be one, too."

The other children agreed that this was fair.

Taking turns, the boys chose their teammates. Bert picked Nellie, Freddie, Susie, and Charlie. Nan, Flossie, Teddy, and Jack were on Danny's side.

The young archers took turns shooting the rubber-tipped arrows. Nellie and Jack proved to be very good shots, but Flossie and Teddy missed the target each time. When all but Danny and Freddie had shot three arrows the score stood even.

"Too bad, Bert," said Danny as he prepared to shoot his last arrow. "This is where your side loses." The arrow flew through the air and landed in the circle nearest the bull's-eye.

Smiling triumphantly, Danny passed the bow and another arrow to Freddie. Adjusting the arrow to the string, the little boy pulled back on it, aimed carefully and released it.

The arrow landed directly on the bull's-eye with a little thump!

"I hit it! We won!" Freddie cried gleefully.

"Good for you!" Bert praised him.

Everyone except Danny clapped.

Freddie beamed proudly as the bully picked up the archery set and put it in the box.

Jack spoke up. "Say, if you kids want to be real Indians, your courage should be tested the way our teacher, Miss Vandermeer, told us."

"That's right," Charlie agreed. "Warriors used to walk on a narrow tree branch across a

The arrow landed directly on the bull's-eye!

rushing river to prove how brave they were."

"But we don't have a river with a tree branch on it," Freddie pointed out.

"We can make a pretend one," Bert spoke up. "How about using a pole stretched between two kitchen stools?"

He went into the house for the stools and a long pole. Returning shortly, he said, "The grass will have to be the river." He arranged the pole with each end tied onto one of the stools.

"I want to go first!" Freddie cried. "I'm the bravest Indian!"

He climbed onto the nearest stool and started across the pole. Stretching out his arms to balance himself, he slid one rubber-soled sneaker very slowly in front of the other.

Freddie had just reached the middle of the pole when Danny slightly kicked the stool nearest him. It shifted, the pole moved, and Freddie lost his balance. He fell to the ground!

"You made him fall, Danny Rugg!" Bert said hotly, doubling up his fists.

"Aw, I didn't do it on purpose," Danny said. "You Bobbseys are a bunch of crybabies! I'll give you something to cry over!"

With that Danny ran full tilt into one of the tepees and knocked it over. Instantly Bert and Charlie made a dash for him, but the bully dodged out of the way, grabbed his archery set and ran quickly from the yard. Jack followed.

"Let them go!" Nellie called to the boys. "Good riddance!"

"Danny alway spoils things!" Nan said.

"I'm glad he's gone," said Flossie, putting her chin up in the air. "Let's forget him and have a war dance!"

With Nan in the lead the children formed a circle and pranced around uttering loud whoops. A few minutes later a car turned into the driveway and a tall, good-looking man got out.

"Daddy!" Flossie cried, dashing across the yard to jump into his arms.

"How's my little fat fairy?" he asked. "I see she's turned into an Indian." Then as Freddie ran up, he laughed. "So has my little fireman!"

These were Mr. Bobbsey's nicknames for the small twins. Ever since Freddie was a very little boy he had wanted to become a fireman.

"Now we can hear the mystery," Bert said excitedly.

The twins waved good-by to their playmates and followed Mr. Bobbsey into the house. They found their mother in the living room. She was a slim, pretty woman. Smiling, she held up two long envelopes. "Are you ready to hear the mystery?" she asked teasingly.

"Oh, yes!"

CHAPTER II

RUNAWAYS

THE twins listened eagerly as their mother began. "This first letter," she explained, "is from a lawyer in Santa Fe, New Mexico. He says my Great-uncle Alan, whom I never knew, has died and left me his cattle ranch."

"A ranch!" Bert exclaimed. "That's keen!"

Nan's eyes danced. "What's the mystery, Mother?"

"That's in the second letter," Mrs. Bobbsey replied. "It's from Tom Yager, the foreman of the Half Circle Ranch. He wants us to come out there because of trouble he's having."

"What kind of trouble?" Nan asked.

"The cattle are disappearing! Only a few at a time, so at first it wasn't noticeable."

"Rustlers?" Bert asked.

"Mr. Yager doesn't know, but he wants us to come as soon as possible."

"I'm ready, Mother," Freddie spoke up. "I want to stop those bad men!"

The Bobbsey twins loved adventure and mystery, and had solved some very exciting cases. In the BOBBSEY TWINS OF LAKEPORT they found the secret of a haunted house, and in their ADVENTURE IN WASHINGTON they recovered a Lakeport scientist's stolen invention. But they had never met any cattle thieves.

"We'll probably do a lot of horseback riding out West," Bert said. "Nan, let's go to Mr. Hixon's stables tomorrow and take another lesson."

"Great! When do we leave on our trip, Mother?"

"Saturday. That's the earliest Daddy can get away."

The next day after school Nan and Bert rode their bicycles out to the riding stable which was at the edge of town. Mr. Hixon was a tall, thin man with a booming voice.

"Hello there!" he called out cheerily. "How are my prize pupils?"

"We're fine," Bert replied. "May we try riding on western saddles today? We're going to New Mexico."

"I'd like to go out West myself," Mr. Hixon said as he began to saddle Bert's horse. "I might be able to find my son," the riding master ended sadly.

"I didn't know you had a son," Nan said in surprise. "How old is he?"

"Well, Bud would be about twenty-five now," Mr. Hixon said. "I haven't seen him since he was fifteen."

The man explained that he and Bud had quarreled after Bud's mother had died, and the boy had run away.

"He was always fond of horses and Western movies," Mr. Hixon went on, "and I kind of figured he'd gone out West and become a cowboy."

By this time both horses were saddled. "Ride around the ring a few times," the instructor directed. "Then when you're used to the western saddles, you can take that dirt road alongside the woods. You're good enough riders to go out by yourselves."

"Oh, thank you," Nan said with a smile.

"A trot won't be comfortable in those saddles," Mr. Hixon added. "Get the horses into a canter, but remember to relax your bodies and keep the balls of your feet firm in the stirrups."

Bert and Nan promised to follow his advice. They took several turns around the outdoor ring at the side of the stables, then guided their horses onto the country road. It was a beautiful June day and the horses stepped along briskly.

"Let's canter," Nan proposed. She gathered

up the reins and touched the horse lightly with her heels. Her mount broke into an easy canter and Bert's followed.

"This is great!" Bert cried as the twins moved forward.

Suddenly a rabbit dashed from the woods and across the road. Nan's horse was startled. Without warning he took the bit between his teeth and began to gallop down the road.

"Stop him, Bert!" screamed Nan. Her feet slipped from the stirrups. As she lost her balance, Nan grabbed the horn on her saddle.

Like a shot Bert urged his horse into a gallop. He pulled up even with Nan, leaned over and grabbed her horse's bridle. The animals galloped a few more paces, then gradually came to a stop.

"Oh thanks, Bert," said Nan. She leaned forward and shakily patted her horse's neck. The animal was still quivering with fright.

"Are you all right?" Bert asked his sister.

Nan nodded and managed a smile. "I guess I didn't have full control of him or he wouldn't have been able to bolt like that."

"At least you stayed on him," Bert replied with a grin. "Let's ride up to the next crossroad and then back to the stable."

When they returned, the twins said nothing to Mr. Hixon about their scare. He took the horses and waved good-by as they pedaled off.

When Bert and Nan reached home they found Freddie and Flossie in the living room entertaining an elderly friend whom they called Aunt Sally Pry. They all loved her, but she had one failing which often amused them. Mrs. Pry was quite deaf but refused to wear a hearing aid. She often made funny mistakes in trying to answer what was said.

The elderly woman was seated on the sofa with a child on either side. She looked up when Bert and Nan came into the room and held out her hands to them.

"I'm glad to see you, my dears," she said. "Where have you been?"

"We've been riding," Nan told her.

"Hiding? Why were you hiding?" Aunt Sally asked in surprise.

Nan smiled and explained to Mrs. Pry.

"Oh!" Aunt Sally said. "I guess I don't hear very well. But be careful of horses."

"Nan's horse bolted today," Bert said, "but between us we stopped him."

"Nan's not old enough to vote," Aunt Sally said severely. "You know that, Bert." The twins found it hard not to giggle.

"The reason I came to see your mother," the elderly woman went on, "is that I learned you're going out West. I'd like to ride as far as Chicago with you. I want to visit my nephew there, and I'm kind of afraid to go alone."

"Stop him, Bert!" screamed Nan

At this moment the front door opened and presently Mrs. Bobbsey walked into the room. When she heard the reason for Mrs. Pry's call, she said, "We'd love to have you with us as far as Chicago. We'll make the arrangements."

"Oh, thank you."

That evening a family conference was held. "We'll travel by train," Mr. Bobbsey said. "In Chicago we'll get on another train for Santa Fe."

"Goody!" said Flossie. "It's fun to sleep on trains!"

The next few days were busy ones. On Friday when Freddie was leaving school, Teddy Blake came up to him. "I've brought you a present to take to the ranch with you," he said.

Teddy pulled a wooden whistle from his pocket. "It makes a lot of noise," he declared. "I thought you could use it if you get lost."

"Thanks," Freddie said. He blew a blast on the toy. "This is neat!"

That afternoon Bert and Nan went out to the stables for a last ride. They told Mr. Hixon they were going West the next day.

"Keep a watch for my son Bud," he said. "If you see him, tell him I'd like mighty well to have him back here."

"How would we know Bud?" Nan asked.

"He's tall, like me, and has his mother's dark curly hair."

"Is there anything unusual about his looks?" Bert inquired.

Mr. Hixon thought a minute. "Well, he had an accident when he was six which left the little finger on his right hand crooked."

"We'll try to find him," Nan promised.

When the ride was over and the twins were on their way home, Nan looked at Bert and said happily, "Now we have two mysteries to solve!"

Sam was to drive the family to the station the next day, where they would meet Aunt Sally Pry. As Mrs. Bobbsey came out of the house and got into the car she looked around. "Where's Flossie?" she asked.

No one had seen the little girl.

"I'll get her!" Freddie jumped from the car and ran into the house.

When he came back with his twin, both children were giggling. Flossie was carrying a straw bag which Susie Larker had given her. It seemed to be heavy.

She climbed into the station wagon next to her mother and carefully put the bag on the seat. Sam started the motor and the station wagon rolled down the driveway.

As they turned into the street, Flossie's straw bag suddenly jumped into the air. A loud meow came from it!

"Flossie!" Mrs. Bobbsey cried. *"What* is in that bag?"

With an impish grin Flossie lifted the lid. Out jumped Snoop, the Bobbseys' black cat!

"I thought Snoop would be lonely while we're away," the little girl explained, "so I was going to carry him in this. But I guess he doesn't like it!"

"There will be lots of animals on the ranch," Mr. Bobbsey told her. "I'm sure Snoop will be happier at home."

Sam chuckled. "I'll take him back. Dinah would be right lonely without Snoop."

When the Bobbseys pulled up to the station platform, Aunt Sally was pacing up and down.

"I'm so glad to see you," she cried. "I was afraid you'd miss the train—I don't know how to make those beds on the sleeping car."

"You won't have to do that," Mrs. Bobbsey said soothingly. "The porter will fix you up."

"Mix me up!" The old lady laughed. "I'm mixed up already."

Just then the train pulled into the station, and Mr. Bobbsey helped Aunt Sally aboard. The others followed.

A smiling porter in a neat white coat carried Mrs. Pry's suitcase into a small room with a seat across the end. "I'll come back after dinner and show you how the bed works," he assured her.

In the meantime the Bobbseys had gone into their accommodations. These were two bedrooms with a long seat in each one and a door which connected the two.

"Daddy and the boys can have one room and you girls and I will take the other," Mrs. Bobbsey announced.

The children ran about, examining everything. Freddie pulled a handle under a mirror and a stainless steel wash basin folded down from the wall.

"This is neat!" he exclaimed. "I think I'll wash my hands!"

Freddie carefully took off his jacket. Several pennies jingled in the pocket so he took them out and placed them on the side of the basin. His hands clean, Freddie looked around. How did the water get out of the basin?

"I guess I'll push it up again and see what happens," he told himself. Quickly he folded the wash basin up into the wall, then pulled it down. The water was gone!

Then suddenly Freddie thought of his pennies. They had disappeared! He got down on his knees and looked around the floor, but the pennies were not there.

Mr. and Mrs. Bobbsey came back into the room and saw their son on the floor. The little boy explained what had happened.

"That's too bad," said his mother, and Mr. Bobbsey added, "You'll have to earn some more pennies to make up for them, Freddie. And now

we're all going to the dining car. Aunt Sally is
ready."

The seven travelers made their way through
several cars until they came to the diner. It
looked very attractive with the fresh white
tablecloths and shining glasses. The tables along
each side of the aisle seated four persons.

"We'll have to divide up," Mr. Bobbsey remarked.

"Freddie and I want to sit with Aunt Sally!"
Flossie begged.

"All right."

The small twins' table was very lively with
Freddie and Flossie changing their minds sev-
eral times about what they wanted to eat and
Aunt Sally misunderstanding the waiter.

"I want a peach sundae!" Flossie announced
when it was time for dessert.

Aunt Sally looked up from the menu. "Go to
the beach Sunday!" she exclaimed. "You can't
do that. You're going to New Mexico!"

Flossie giggled and made motions of eating
ice cream. "A peach sundae," she repeated.

Aunt Sally laughed. "There I go again! Of
course you may have a peach sundae!"

Later that evening when the Bobbseys were
tired and getting ready for bed, they suddenly
heard a loud shriek from one of the roomettes.

"Help! Help!"

CHAPTER III

STRANDED!

THE cry was coming from Aunt Sally's roomette! Mr. and Mrs. Bobbsey dashed into the corridor, followed by the twins. Their father threw open the door of the roomette.

Aunt Sally stood there, both hands outstretched, holding up a wall bed which was about to come forward. "Help!" she cried. "This thing is falling on top of me!"

Mr. Bobbsey jumped to her side. "Just step back, Aunt Sally," he said calmly. "I'll pull down this berth."

Fearfully, Mrs. Pry let go and went to stand with the others in the doorway. Mr. Bobbsey lowered the bed until it dropped into place.

"Well, I declare!" Aunt Sally cried. "Who'd ever expect a bed to come from the wall? I just reached up to see what those handles were for and the thing started falling on me!"

"Trains are fun!" Flossie piped up. "Our beds come down from the wall too!"

"It's too late to play ball." Aunt Sally shook her head. "I'm going to bed."

Flossie started to explain what she had said, then changed her mind. She kissed Aunt Sally good night and ran back to her own room.

Nan and Flossie climbed into their upper berth and were soon fast asleep. When they awakened the next morning the train was passing through the Chicago suburbs.

"Hurry and dress, girls," Mrs. Bobbsey called. "We'll be at the station in ten minutes."

They climbed down and hastily put on their clothes. The porter came for the luggage, and Mr. Bobbsey met them in the corridor.

"We'll have breakfast in the station," he said. "I've arranged for a car to meet us afterward and drive us around the city for some sightseeing."

Aunt Sally's nephew was waiting for her, and she said good-by to the Bobbseys. "You must come to see me when you get back to Lakeport and tell me all about the ranch," she said.

The children promised, then followed their parents into the restaurant.

As the Bobbseys were finishing breakfast a man in a chauffeur's uniform came to their table. "The car you ordered is parked outside," he said. "I'll take you whenever you're ready."

"Fine," said Mr. Bobbsey. "We're all set."

Since it was Sunday there was not much traffic

on the streets of the big city. The car drove along the attractive boulevard which bordered Lake Michigan. The children were surprised to see sandy beaches just across the road from huge apartment houses.

"Can't we stop and go swimming?" Freddie begged.

"I'm afraid not," Mr. Bobbsey replied. "We'll just have time for a drive around the city and some lunch before our train leaves."

The driver stopped at a charming restaurant overlooking the lake. Then, after a hearty meal, they headed back for the station.

"When will we reach the ranch?" Bert asked.

"We should be there late tomorrow afternoon," his father replied. "This train doesn't usually stop at Vinton, which is the town nearest the ranch. But as long as there are six passengers to get off, it will stop for us tomorrow."

Freddie grinned as they boarded the train. "I'm going to look for cowboys tomorrow!" he declared.

But in the morning he did not notice any cowboys. On either side of the tracks fields of grain stretched as far as the eye could see.

Flossie pressed her nose against the glass. "Who's going to eat all this?" she asked.

"Oh, you and I and lots of other people," Nan replied.

Late in the morning the twins heard the conductor call out something. "What's he saying?" Flossie asked.

Bert stepped into the corridor. He came back shortly. "We're going to stop at a station and will be there in about ten minutes. May we get off, Dad?"

"Yes, I think you all need to stretch your legs. But don't go far away from the train. You must be ready to get on again as soon as the conductor calls, 'All aboard.'"

"Come on!" Freddie urged, running out of the roomette. "We're slowing down now."

The train ground to a halt and the four children jumped to the station platform. They seemed to be at the edge of a small town. Groups of curious people stood staring at the train while large mail sacks were brought up on hand trucks.

"I'm going to buy some peppermints," Nan declared, walking over to a candy counter in the little station. Flossie trailed along.

Bert and Freddie strolled up to the front of the train to admire the engine. The engineer was standing nearby, and Bert began to ask him questions. Soon the two were deep in conversation.

Freddie listened for a few minutes, then turned back to find Flossie. As he walked along the platform he saw three boys crouched on the ground near the station building. They were playing marbles.

Freddie walked over to them. The youngest boy, who seemed to be about Freddie's age, looked up. "Want to play?" he asked in a friendly manner.

"Yes," Freddie said, "but I haven't any marbles with me."

"Here." The strange boy pushed a handful over to Freddie. "I'll lend you some."

Freddie knelt down. "Thanks," he said. A moment later he was deep in the game. The shooter which the boy had given him seemed to be lucky. In a short time Freddie had won almost all the other marbles.

He was just shooting for the last ones in the circle when he happened to look up. The train was moving! As Freddie watched, horrified, it began to pick up speed.

"Hey! Wait!" the little boy shouted, running up the platform after the train.

A brakeman standing at the end of the last car caught sight of Freddie and heard his cries. Quickly he pulled the emergency cord. The train screeched to a stop.

"Th-thank you!" Freddie panted as the brakeman helped him up the steps of the car.

"You almost got left that time, sonny!" the man said sternly. "Didn't you hear the conductor call, 'All aboard'?"

Freddie looked sheepish. "No, sir," he said. "I'm sorry. I was playing with some boys."

At that moment Bert dashed into the car.

"What happened, Freddie?" he asked. "Did the train stop for you just now? When I couldn't find you, I thought you'd climbed back on."

The little boy explained.

Bert grinned. "You were lucky," he said. "You'd have had a long walk to New Mexico."

Some time after the Bobbseys had eaten lunch the conductor knocked on their door. "We'll be in Vinton in ten minutes, Mr. Bobbsey," he announced. "The porter will take your bags now."

Mr. and Mrs. Bobbsey and the twins picked up their belongings and waited at the end of the car until the train stopped. Then they hurried down the steps. In a few moments the train pulled away.

As the Bobbseys looked around, a flashily dressed cowboy came up to them. Freddie's eyes opened wide in excitement as he gazed at the embroidered jacket and ten-gallon hat.

Around his slim waist the man wore a wide leather belt trimmed in silver and fastened with a large silver buckle. His boots were leather inlaid with pieces of a contrasting color and stitched in an intricate pattern. The heels were higher than Freddie had seen before on men's shoes.

"Mr. and Mrs. Bobbsey?" the man asked.

When the twins' father nodded, the cowboy

"Hey, wait!" Freddie shouted

continued, "I'm Jones. I'll drive you to the Half
Circle Ranch."

Before Mr. Bobbsey could say anything, the
man picked up the biggest suitcases and led the
way toward a dilapidated-looking station wagon

parked beside the small station. Mr. Bobbsey and Bert took the rest of the luggage.

"Is it very far to the ranch?" Mrs. Bobbsey asked as they started off.

Jones muttered something no one could hear and started the motor. He drove at a fast clip down what seemed to be the main street of the town.

The Bobbseys could see a few stores, a restaurant, and a small hotel. Jones looked neither right nor left and did not volunteer any information.

"Isn't the scenery lovely?" Mrs. Bobbsey remarked, gazing at the distant mountainside covered with wild flowers.

"And there are some more cowboys!" Nan cried as two young men came out of a building. They wore tight blue denim trousers, plaid shirts, and wide-brimmed felt hats. The children turned around to watch as the men got into a jeep and roared off.

In a short time the station wagon had left the town and was bumping along a narrow dirt road. The land was flat but surrounded by mountains.

Nan took a deep breath. "Isn't the air fresh?" she exclaimed happily.

The road ran in a straight line toward the far-off mountains. Cattle grazed peacefully in the distance.

After half an hour Mrs. Bobbsey asked uneasily, "Aren't we almost to the ranch, Mr. Jones? I understood from the foreman that it was only about ten miles from Vinton."

The cowboy at the wheel grunted but did not reply. Instead he pointed vaguely ahead. A few minutes later he turned onto a rutted road, drove for a few miles, then turned again through a broken-down gateway.

He stopped before an old frame house, badly in need of paint, and turned off the motor.

"Is this the Half Circle Ranch?" Mr. Bobbsey asked in surprise.

The man nodded. He stepped from the car and began to take the luggage from the back. The children scrambled out and ran toward the house. Mr. and Mrs. Bobbsey looked at each other in dismay and walked after them.

Nan had stepped onto the sagging porch of the house and peered into a window. "This place is deserted!" she exclaimed. "It can't be the right one!"

They all turned to question the cowboy. He had driven off!

CHAPTER IV

SMOKE SIGNAL

"WAIT!" Bert shouted. He dashed down the road after the cowboy.

But Jones paid no attention and in a few minutes all that could be seen of the station wagon was a little puff of dust on the horizon.

The Bobbseys looked at one another in dismay. What could they do? They were miles from town with no sign of any house near them.

"Whose big idea was this?" Bert asked, as he turned back to the others. No one had an answer. The family was completely mystified.

"Let's look in the house," Nan proposed. "Maybe we can find a clue."

The front door opened easily when the girl pushed it. They all stepped inside. The place had obviously been vacant for some time. There were no shades at the windows and no rugs on the floor. The few pieces of furniture were broken.

"This is weird," Bert remarked as he walked

into what had once been a comfortable kitchen. A few empty food tins littered the floor. In one corner was a pile of old feed catalogs.

"Are we going to stay here, Daddy?" Flossie wailed. "I don't like it!"

"I don't either!" her father said. "But you'll all have to make the best of it while I go for help."

"But Dick," Mrs. Bobbsey protested, "it's too far to walk to town and we didn't pass anyone on the road!"

Bert had been looking around thoughtfully. Now he spoke up. "I have an idea! The Indians used to send up smoke signals when they wanted to communicate with other Indians. Why can't we do that?"

"You mean build a fire and hope someone sees the smoke?" Nan asked, looking more cheerful.

"Yes!"

"A good idea, son," said his father. "Let's get busy!"

They decided to build the fire in front of the house. The children scurried around picking up anything which would burn.

Flossie carried out several of the catalogs and Nan found a broken stool. Bert contributed an old rocker. He and his father began to pile the odds and ends onto the crumpled-up seed catalogs.

"This is all dry wood," Mr. Bobbsey commented. "It should make a good fire."

"I hope it sends up a lot of smoke," Bert added.

Freddie had wandered out the back door and over to a tumble-down shed. He spied an old tire casing. "I'll put that on the fire," he decided.

When Freddie pulled the tire casing around the corner of the house, Bert gave a whoop.

"Good for you, Freddie! That's just the thing to make smoke!" Freddie beamed proudly.

Mr. Bobbsey placed lighted matches among the papers and in a short while the fire was burning briskly. Bert threw the rubber tire on the top. It smoldered there, throwing a column of smoke straight up into the still air.

"That's all we can do now," Mr. Bobbsey remarked. "We'll just have to wait. Let's hope your smoke signal works, Bert, and somebody rescues us."

For the next half hour Mr. and Mrs. Bobbsey sat on the step of the sagging porch and talked while the twins explored the place. There was not much to see. The house was empty except for the odds and ends of broken furniture. The yard around the house yielded nothing more interesting.

Suddenly Flossie called out, "Someone's coming!"

"I hope it sends up a lot of smoke," Bert said

The others peered down the road. A cloud of
dust came nearer and finally they could make
out a jeep speeding toward them.

A minute later it stopped at the gate and a

short, middle-aged man got out. "I'm Zeke Dawkins," he drawled. "You folks in trouble?"

When Mr. Bobbsey explained what had happened, the man exclaimed, "Well, that shore is a shame. Don't know why that feller brought you here! The Half Circle Ranch is away on the other side of Vinton!"

"Did you see the smoke from our fire, Mr. Dawkins?" Freddie interrupted eagerly. "I found the tire that made it!"

"That was a very smart idea, young feller," Dawkins said. "Kirby up at the fire tower saw it and radioed me to find out what was up. I'm a volunteer fire fighter."

Their rescuer told the Bobbseys that fire towers were located on the mountains. A watcher stayed in each tower to look for fires, especially in wooded areas, and report them. Then volunteers in the surrounding country were notified by short-wave radio and they would rush to the spot to fight the fire.

"I'd like to be a fire watcher," Freddie declared, secretly wishing he had brought his toy engine.

"Can you get in touch with Tom Yager, the foreman, and ask him to come for us?" Mrs. Bobbsey inquired.

"I'll do better than that," Dawkins replied. "I'll take you all into Vinton and you can call

Tom from there. That's much nearer the Half Circle."

With relief and laughter the six Bobbseys squeezed themselves and their luggage into the jeep and Dawkins drove off.

Bert and Nan sat in front. "Have you ever met a man by the name of Bud Hixon?" Nan asked the driver. "He may have come West from Lakeport." She explained about Mr. Hixon and his missing son.

Dawkins thought a minute, then shook his head. "Can't say as I ever heard that name," he said. "But there's a cowboy on the Half Circle Ranch who came from the East. Maybe he knows this Hixon."

"What's the cowboy's name?" Bert asked.

"Bill Dayton. He's a nice fellow."

It was dark by the time they reached the town of Vinton. Dawkins stopped the jeep in front of the hotel. The sign over the door said, "The Frontier House."

"You can get a good meal in here while you're waiting for Tom," Dawkins suggested. Then he spoke quickly to Nan, "There's Bill Dayton now!"

A tall, thin young man in cowboy garb was just passing under the street light.

Bert jumped from the jeep. "Mr. Dayton!" he called.

Without turning, the cowboy hurried on and disappeared around a corner.

"Guess he didn't hear you," Dawkins remarked.

The Bobbseys thanked the man for his help and walked into the hotel.

"You children go on into the dining room while your mother and I call the ranch," Mr. Bobbsey directed.

When the children entered the restaurant the first thing they saw was a long, lighted window set into one wall. Inside the boxlike frame was a miniature covered wagon pulled by six tiny horses.

"Isn't it darling!" Nan exclaimed.

"See the little people!" Flossie cried, pointing out several figures which were placed as if walking beside the wagon. The leader, who held a tiny whip, seemed to be urging the horses to go faster.

A smiling waitress walked up to the children. "Do you like our diorama?" she asked. "You'll see many of these scenic displays in the West."

"It's bee-yoo-ti-ful!" Flossie exclaimed.

The waitress showed the twins to a large table, and in a few minutes their parents joined them.

"Is Tom Yager coming for us?" Bert asked when they had ordered.

"Yes," his mother replied. "He'll bring his

big car so there'll be room for all of us and the luggage." She added in a puzzled tone, "Something is very odd. Tom says someone telegraphed him that we wouldn't arrive until day after tomorrow."

"The message you sent him must have been mixed up," Mr. Bobbsey observed.

Tom Yager came a half hour later. The Bobbseys immediately liked the tall, sandyhaired foreman. He held himself very erect and walked with a rolling gait.

"Howdy, folks!" he greeted Mr. and Mrs. Bobbsey and the twins with a broad grin.

He led them to a vehicle parked at the curb. It was a large gray car with the usual two long seats. Back of the second seat two others ran the length of the car on either side.

"This is neat!" Bert said admiringly, helping Tom and his father pile the luggage into the back.

In a few minutes they had left the town and were driving out into the country.

"How near the stars seem!" Nan exclaimed, gazing up into the sky. "They look as if you could almost touch them!"

"That's because the air is so clear," her father told her. "There's no smoke to mar the view."

"And it's so quiet!" Flossie observed. "It's spooky!"

Tom Yager explained that the Half Circle Ranch was located in a green valley between two ranges of mountains. "You can't ride far without getting into the hills," he told them.

At that moment he turned through a gateway into a narrow road. A mile or so farther on, he stopped the car in front of a low, rambling building. Vines grew over the porch which stretched across the front.

"Welcome to Half Circle!" the foreman exclaimed as he helped Mrs. Bobbsey from the car. "Most everyone's gone to bed, but you'll meet 'em all in the morning."

When the Bobbseys entered the big living room of the ranch house, a tall boy with curly blond hair came to greet them. He appeared to be about sixteen years old.

"This is my son Wes," said Tom. "Mrs. Yager is in California visiting her mother. She is sorry to miss you."

"We're glad to have you here," Wes said with a friendly smile. "Dad says I'm to show you around."

"And this is our cook, Sing Foo," the foreman said as a short, fat Chinese with a jolly smile came into the room. He wore black trousers and a neat white jacket and was carrying a tray.

"Good evening," Sing Foo said, bowing

deeply. "I think maybe you like some refreshment."

He placed the tray on a nearby table, then poured coffee for Mr. and Mrs. Bobbsey and tall glasses of creamy milk for the children. Next the cook passed a plate of cookies.

"These rice cakes are Sing Foo's specialty," Tom said.

"They're yummy!" Flossie cried as she took a large bite of hers.

While the Bobbseys were enjoying the snack, Wes and his father brought in the luggage and carried it to the three bedrooms which had been prepared for the visitors.

When the Yagers rejoined the others, the foreman said, "We'll show you around the ranch tomorrow. I imagine you're all tired now."

Just then Freddie pointed a finger toward the window and cried, "L-look! Indians!"

CHAPTER V

A QUICK LASSO

FOUR dark, piercing eyes stared in through the kitchen window!

Just as Freddie ran into the next room, Sing Foo remarked, "Oh, they niece and nephew of Johnny Bat. He ride fence for Half Circle." The Chinese cook invited the Indian girl and boy inside.

Freddie grinned. "Hi!" he said.

All four twins liked Rainbow and River Deer, who were about ten. They thought Rainbow looked very cute in her leather-fringed dress and her black hair in braids. River Deer wore trousers and a long overblouse with a dangling silver necklace made of discs as large as half dollars.

"We hear you come," Rainbow said a bit shyly. "We come ask you visit our reservation. Will you?"

"Will we!" shouted Freddie. "You bet!"

The others also accepted the invitation, saying they would come soon. The Indian children left.

"Do they go home in the dark?" Flossie asked, worried.

"Yes, missy," said Sing Foo. "Indians never need flashlights. They see and hear very well in dark."

Before the visitors said good night to the ranchers, Mrs. Bobbsey turned to Tom Yager. "I'd like to hear more about the disappearing cattle. Have you learned the cause?"

"Yes," Tom answered. "We've been plagued by rustlers."

"Rustlers!" Bert exclaimed. "Just like in the movies!"

"Tell us about it, Tom," Mrs. Bobbsey urged.

"Well, you see," Yager began, "the Half Circle is what's called an enclosed ranch; that is, our grazing areas are fenced in. There are two large acreages which we call the north range and the south range. Cattle have disappeared from both."

"Of course you have reported this to the sheriff?" Mr. Bobbsey spoke up.

Tom nodded. "Yes. Sheriff Werner and his deputies have been trying to catch the thieves, but they haven't had any luck so far."

"Maybe we can find the rustlers," Bert said excitedly.

Seeing Tom's startled look, Mr. Bobbsey smiled. "Our children are pretty good at solving mysteries," he said. "They may be able to unravel this one."

"I'd be mightily obliged if they could," Tom declared earnestly.

"You twins have two weeks to do the job," their father teased.

Talk turned to the Bobbseys' strange experience at the deserted house.

"Do you know the cowboy who met us at the train?" Nan asked Tom Yager.

"What did he look like?" the foreman inquired.

Bert described the flashily dressed stranger. At the mention of the man's fancy shoes, Wes exclaimed:

"He sounds like Boots! But Dad, why would Boots play a trick like that?"

"You've got me!"

The foreman explained that Boots, whose last name was not Jones but Harris, had ridden for the Half Circle Ranch at one time. He had become dissatisfied after a while and had left.

"The other hands called him Boots because he spent all his money having fancy boots made for himself," Wes went on. "He sure liked to spread the mustard!" The boy grinned and added, "I mean, he liked to put on airs!"

By this time the small twins were almost asleep in their chairs. Mrs. Bobbsey insisted they go to bed.

That night Freddie dreamed he was a fire fighter. He was just about to put out a big fire when a train came by and dumped a bag of marbles on the blaze. At that moment he woke up to find the sun streaming in the window and Bert dressing.

"Hurry up, sleepyhead," his brother said. "They ring a bell here for meals and the breakfast bell just rang."

When the hearty meal was over, Mrs. Bobbsey said to the twins, "I think we should wear western clothes while we're here on the ranch. Wes says he can drive us into town to do some shopping."

"Goody!" said Flossie. "I want a cowgirl suit!"

An hour later Wes parked at a small store on the main street of Vinton. The twins hurried inside.

"Ooh, look at all the clothes!" Flossie exclaimed.

Every inch of the store was filled with western equipment. Tables were piled high with blue jeans and stacks of shirts. Felt hats hung on racks along the walls. At the rear of the store were seats for people trying on boots.

A pleasant-looking woman came forward to help the newcomers. In a short time Freddie and Flossie were outfitted and wandered to the boot department.

"Let's play shoe store," Flossie proposed. "You fit me with cowgirl boots." She sat down on a chair.

Freddie, grinning, picked up a pair from a shelf, sat down on a stool, and slipped a boot over his twin's right foot. The boot was tight and he had to work to get it on.

"Ouch! It pinches!" Flossie cried. "Take it off!"

Her brother pulled, but the boot would not budge. As he gave an extra hard tug, she screamed. "That hurts!"

The other Bobbseys and the clerk hurried over.

"What's the matter?" the woman asked.

Flossie explained and Bert said, "I'll help get it off." He knelt behind Freddie and put his arms around him. "Now we'll pull together!" he said.

The boys gave a mighty yank. The next instant Flossie was pulled from the chair and her brothers toppled backward!

"Oh!" the little girl squealed. But Flossie's foot was free!

Mrs. Bobbsey laughed and asked the clerk to show Flossie a pair of boots in the right size.

The boys gave a mighty yank and toppled backward!

Soon she was fitted properly, and then Freddie got a pair.

While waiting, Nan asked the clerk about the strange cowboy.

"Boots? No. He doesn't come here."

Nan was disappointed and wondered where she could learn more about him.

As the family was gathering up their purchases, Wes spoke up. "Maybe you'd better have saddle slickers in case you get caught while riding in the rain."

"What are they?" Bert asked.

Wes explained that the slickers were made to cover the saddle as well as the rider. They were rolled and tied behind the saddle for emergency use.

After buying the slickers, Mrs. Bobbsey picked out bright silk mufflers for all of them. "Tom told me to be sure to get these," she said. "They can be pulled up over the mouth and nose to keep out the dust."

As soon as they returned to the ranch the twins hurried to put on their new clothes. Flossie patted her denims and giggled. "I feel like a real cowgirl!"

In a few minutes she and the other children went out to the corral to look at the horses. A cowboy came up to them. He had straight black hair and piercing dark eyes. "Hi-ya," he said pleasantly. "I'm Johnny Bat. I'll be glad to show you anything you want to know about ridin' or ropin'."

"Are you an Indian?" Freddie asked.

Johnny laughed. "You bet."

Freddie popped up. "We have Indian names too. Bert's is Roman Nose. I'm Little Wolf."

"You are my brothers!" Johnny solemnly shook hands with the boys.

"I guess we're your sisters," Nan said with a chuckle. "Flossie's Jumping Rabbit and I'm Singing Brook."

Johnny raised one arm in the air. "How, sister!" he said and everyone giggled.

The cowboy turned toward the corral. "How about me catchin' you some horses?"

The children nodded eagerly and watched with interest as Johnny saddled two palominos and tied them to the corral fence. Then from the far side of the enclosure he brought two smaller brown-and-white mottled horses.

"These here are Indian ponies," he explained. "They'll do fine for Freddie and Flossie."

When the ponies were saddled, Johnny helped the small twins mount. Bert and Nan were already in the saddle. For the next half hour the cowboy took the children around an open field near the corral.

"Bert and Nan," he said when the twins finally slid from their saddles, "you're pretty good. You handle your horses well. And all the young'uns need is more practice."

Bert brought up the subject of the missing cattle. The Indian frowned. "Bad business. I hope no more will disappear."

Johnny went back to his work, and the twins wandered over to a fenced-in field where several cows and calves were grazing.

Freddie stood by the fence, his hands in his pockets. His fingers closed over the whistle Teddy Blake had given him. Absentmindedly, Freddie took it out and blew a shrill blast.

Suddenly, every cow and calf in the field panicked. They began running around and mooing and maa-ing loudly. One calf with a white star on her forehead made a beeline toward Freddie, leaping into the air every few seconds.

"Ow!" the little boy squealed, and started to dash for the ranch house.

The frightened calf jumped high and cleared the fence. It kept on loping after Freddie.

By this time the cries of the other children had alerted Johnny. He came running, grabbed a rope from a nail on the fence, and raced after the calf. Twirling the rope in a large loop, he tossed it high.

"Yippee!" shouted Bert as the rope settled

neatly over the calf and was drawn tightly to trip the animal.

Everyone rushed forward to Johnny's side. He picked up the calf in his strong arms, saying, "Little gal, you sure are a frisky one. You'd better stay with your mommy." He put the calf over the fence. Johnny grinned at Freddie. "Don't think you ought to use that there stampede whistle o' yours around here again." Freddie promised not to except in an emergency.

Flossie ran over to the chicken yard. Sing Foo was there throwing feed to the clucking hens.

"You want help feed chickens, little girl?" the cook asked with a broad smile. "I show you Jenny."

"Who's Jenny?" Flossie asked.

Sing Foo made a high chirping noise. At the sound a fat gray hen ran up to him. The Chinese bent over and the hen jumped onto his arm. She sat there, her beady eyes blinking rapidly.

"Oh! May I hold Jenny?" Flossie cried.

The cook carefully put out his arm and the hen jumped onto Flossie's shoulder.

"Ooh! She tickles!" Flossie exclaimed.

At that moment a short, stocky cowboy came along. He glared at the cook and the little girl.

"Haven't you anything better to do, Sing Foo?" he said scornfully. "These dudes are up-settin' the whole ranch!" He went into the bunk-house and slammed the door.

Flossie's blue eyes filled with tears. "I didn't mean to upset anything," she said.

"Don't you mind, little missy," Sing Foo con-soled her. "That Del Logan, he thinks he is big-ger than he is!"

At the dinner table that noon Bert suddenly remembered something and asked if he might talk to Bill Dayton.

"Bill isn't here," Wes said sadly. "He quit about a week ago."

"We wanted to ask him some questions." Nan explained about the missing Bud Hixon. "Do you know where Mr. Dayton is?"

Wes said that Bill had built himself a cabin in the hills where he used to spend holidays. "I think he was going there to stay for a while."

"May we go to see him?" Bert asked.

"Sure," Wes replied. "It's an easy ride from here. I'll take you if Dad says it's all right." Tom Yager nodded his consent.

Sing Foo had been serving the food. Now he spoke up. "You go see Bill. I send him rice cakes."

After dinner Mr. and Mrs. Bobbsey went with Tom on a tour of the ranch. The twins followed Wes out to the corral. He showed

Bert and Nan how to saddle their horses and then got the ponies ready for Freddie and Flossie.

Just as the five were about to set off, Sing Foo ran from the house with a cardboard box. He held it up to Wes. "Here are rice cakes for Bill," the cook said proudly. "He always like these."

Wes fastened the box to his saddle horn, then led the twins down the ranch road and through the gate. On either side the children saw mountains, some heavily wooded, others brown, with sparse growth of trees.

"The trees are mostly evergreens," Wes explained. "There are some cottonwoods along the streams."

The horses were moving at an easy pace. "We'll take it sort of slow until you get used to western riding," the ranch boy went on, "or else you'll be grabbin' the apple."

Flossie giggled. "I don't see any apples!"

Wes laughed. "That's Western talk. I mean you'll lose your balance and grab the saddle horn."

The group rode across the green valley and up into the hills. Here the going was harder and the children watched carefully to see that their horses did not step into any holes.

Finally after about an hour's ride, Wes pointed to a group of cottonwoods ahead.

"Bill's cabin is among those trees," he said.

As the riders drew nearer they could see a small cabin through the trees. Next to it was a simple two-sided shelter which Wes explained was for Bill's horse.

"I guess he's not at home. His horse is gone," Nan commented.

"Looks that way," Wes agreed. "We'll put the box of cookies inside the cabin."

The children dismounted and hitched their horses to trees. Wes handed the rice cakes to Flossie to hold while he checked to see that the animals were secure.

The twins walked up to the cabin. On the closed door was a printed sign.

BEWARE! FIERCE DOG!

CHAPTER VI

MASKED COWBOY

"OOH!" Flossie squealed. "Let's go away!"

"Bill didn't have a dog when he rode for us," Wes mused. "He must have bought one after he came here to stay."

At that moment the door of the cabin burst open. A large, shaggy black dog sprang out. The children fled in all directions!

Flossie, in her haste to escape, tripped on a tree root and fell. The cake box flew from her hand and the cookies scattered on the ground!

At once the big dog galloped over. The children watched, fascinated, as he gobbled up the sweets. When they were gone, he stood quietly, licking his chops and wagging his tail!

"I don't think he's so fierce!" Bert declared, and walked over to the animal.

The dog jumped, put his big paws on the boy's shoulders and gave him a friendly lick!

The twins gathered around the animal. His

tail wagged vigorously as they patted him.

"You're a smart dog, being able to open doors," Nan remarked.

Wes peered into the cabin, but Bill Dayton was not there. The ranch boy coaxed the dog back inside and hurried out, closing the door.

"I hope Bill guesses the dog ate the cakes Sing Foo sent!" Flossie said, as they mounted their horses and started back to the ranch.

The others laughed, although Bert felt puzzled about the "Fierce Dog" sign. Why had Bill Dayton put it up?

The next morning after breakfast Mr. and Mrs. Bobbsey went into the ranch office to talk business with Tom Yager. Bert looked around for Wes but learned that the boy had ridden out early with some of the cowhands to mend fences.

"Let's go to Bill's cabin again anyway," Bert proposed.

"Do you think we can find the place without Wes?" Nan asked doubtfully.

"Oh, sure," her twin replied. "It isn't far. We just have to watch those woods."

Freddie and Flossie begged to go, so Nan and Bert said all right. Nan, not wishing to disturb her mother, wrote a note to say where they were going and put it on the living room mantel.

None of the ranch hands was at the corral, so Bert and Nan found the two horses and the

Indian ponies they had ridden the day before
and saddled them. In a short time the four
Bobbseys were on their way.

They rode briskly out of the gate as before,
and turned toward the mountain range at the
western edge of the valley.

A half hour later Nan reined up. "It seems
to me we should have reached Bill's cabin by
this time," she said. "Are you sure we're going
in the right direction, Bert?"

Her twin looked around. It was not so easy
to find the place as he had thought. The
mountainside looked the same everywhere, with
no distinguishing marks. They had come to several groves of cottonwoods, but Bill's cabin
was nowhere in sight.

"Are we lost?" Flossie asked.

Nan peered nervously at the sky. It was
covered with black clouds, and a brisk wind
had sprung up.

"I think it's going to rain," she said. "I wish
we could find some kind of shelter."

"We have our slickers," Bert reminded her.
He took the roll from behind his saddle and
began to put it on. The others did the same.

"These are neat!" Freddie exclaimed as he
saw how the waterproof coat protected him as
well as the horn and the saddle.

There were a few drops, then the rain began coming down hard. The twins pulled their

hats lower over their heads and drew their kerchiefs up close around their necks.

Hunched forward against the driving rain, they rode on in silence. Suddenly Freddie cried out, "I see a cabin. Maybe it's Bill's!"

The twins urged their horses on and reined up shortly in front of a small shack. It was not Bill's! The cabin, perched at the edge of a gully, looked shabby. The door was closed.

"I'm sure whoever owns this place won't mind if we take shelter here," Bert said, swinging out of his saddle and tying his horse to a tree. The others also climbed down.

Bert knocked on the door. When there was no answer he pushed it open and they all walked in. Nobody was inside, but there were signs that someone did live in the one-room shack.

In a far corner was an old camp bed with a tattered blanket folded on it. In another corner the children saw a rusty hot plate. A scarred wooden table stood in the center of the room with a battered rocking chair next to it.

The twins took off their slickers and mopped their wet faces with the scarves. Then they began to look around the room.

Bert picked up an iron rod about two feet long from the cot. Another piece of iron was fastened to one end of it.

"What's that?" Freddie asked, as his brother turned it up so the others could see the end.

"Maybe it's a branding iron," Nan said

Here the iron was bent to form a circle with a short bar in the center.

"Maybe it's a branding iron," Nan said slowly. "Remember, Tom showed us the half circle brand on the ranch cattle. He said the mark was burned on with an iron like this."

"I think you're right, Sis," Bert agreed. "But what's it doing here?"

Nan had paused by the table. Now she bent over to examine a map which lay there. "Look!" she exclaimed. "This shows the Half Circle Ranch! And the grazing ranges are marked in pencil!"

Bert peered at the map. "That's queer," he muttered. Then he straightened up, an excited look on his face. "Do you think these things could belong to cattle rustlers? If so, maybe we've found the first clue to the mystery!"

Freddie ran up to the table holding a small wad of paper. "I found this in the corner," he said. "There's writing on it."

Bert took the paper, smoothed it out and read: "Meet at covered wagon—" The rest of the message had been torn off.

"Another clue?" Nan cried. "We'll have to work fast to find the rustlers. You know Dad said he could only be out here two weeks!"

"But people don't ride in covered wagons any more, do they?" Flossie asked, still thinking of the note.

"No," Nan replied. "When the railroads were built across our country, the wagons weren't necessary. Perhaps the note refers to one in a museum."

"This is all very strange," Bert declared. Then, looking out, he reported that the rain had stopped. "We'd better be getting back."

"If we can ride to a high spot, maybe we can see the ranch," Nan suggested.

Accordingly, the twins made their way up to a ridge back of the shack. From there they could look over the green valley. To their surprise, the Half Circle buildings were just below them.

"We must have been traveling in a circle," Bert punned, grinning, as they turned their horses homeward.

When the youngsters rode up to the corral some time later, Mr. Bobbsey was there to meet them. He looked worried.

"I don't want you children riding out without Wes," he said firmly.

Somewhat sheepishly, the twins promised not to set off alone again. Freddie stopped at the fenced-in field and looked for the calf with the star.

"I'm going to call her Star," he decided.

He thought he recognized the calf among the grazing cattle.

"Star!" Freddie yelled. "Come here!"

The calf looked over, then slowly walked to the fence but did not jump over. Freddie was delighted. "We're real pals," he said, stroking the animal's head.

That evening Tom Yager told the Bobbseys that there was to be a local rodeo in Vinton the next afternoon. "Johnny Bat's going to be in it," he said. "Would you like to go?"

"Yippee!" Freddie shouted. "A Wild West rodeo!"

Mr. Bobbsey smiled and said, "I guess you have your answer, Tom!"

The next day after midday dinner, Tom drove the station wagon to the house and everyone piled in. When they reached the outskirts of Vinton, Tom turned into the gate leading to the rodeo grounds.

Suddenly Freddie cried out, "There's a covered wagon!"

"Yes," Tom said. "That's supposed to be the first wagon that reached Vinton in frontier days."

Bert at once thought of the note which Freddie had found in the shack. "I'll keep an eye on this place," he told himself, "But I'd better not say anything until we have more clues."

Handbills were passed to everyone entering the grounds. They announced a special attraction. The "Masked Cowboy" would compete in the bareback bronc-riding contest.

"Doesn't it sound 'citing?" Flossie asked, her eyes shining in anticipation.

A band was playing and the pennants waved from the posts as the group from the Half Circle Ranch took their seats. The bleachers were on one side of the field. Across from them were six pens with gates which could be raised and lowered.

"Those are called chutes," Wes told the twins.

Tom Yager explained that there were five major events in the rodeo. They were saddle-bronc riding, calf roping, bulldogging—or steer wrestling, wild-steer riding and bareback bronc-riding.

"The masked rider is competing in the last event," the foreman said.

"A masked cowboy! Do you know who he is?" Freddie asked.

Wes shook his head. "He'll have to be good to win that bronc-riding contest. There are a lot of great riders around here."

Just then a bugle sounded and the rodeo began. The children stood up and cheered as Johnny Bat won the calf-roping event. First he lassoed the calf, jumped from his horse, threw the animal and tied it, all in the fast time of twenty seconds!

"He's super!" Bert exclaimed.

A cowboy from a neighboring ranch won

the bulldogging event. This meant jumping from his horse, grabbing a steer by the horns and throwing it down.

Wes told the children that these events were judged by the amount of time it took the cowboy to finish. "But the riding contests are judged by points," he concluded.

Finally it was time for the last event, the bareback bronc-riding. One of the chutes opened and a cowboy rode out from the pen on a bucking horse. A red kerchief covered the rider's face up to his eyes. He held the reins in his left hand and waved his hat in his right.

The crowd cheered as the horse almost seemed to bend double. The masked rider kept his seat.

"He's going to get hurt!" Nan cried out.

The horse continued trying to dislodge his rider. Finally one particularly hard buck sent the cowboy flying through the air. He landed face down on the ground.

The people in the stands rose and watched breathlessly. The rider seemed to be stunned, but in a second he got to his feet. The announcement over the loudspeaker said he had the most points and was proclaimed the winner.

As the cowboy turned toward the stands to acknowledge the thunderous applause, he snatched the handkerchief from his face.

"It's Bill Dayton!" Wes shouted.

CHAPTER VII

SUCAMAGROWL

"BILL Dayton!" Nan exclaimed. "Let's go talk to him!"

Wes put out his hand to stop her as she got up. "Wait!" he said. "We can't leave our seats before the prizes are given out."

"What kind of prizes?" Freddie asked.

Wes told the twins that the usual awards given at rodeos were pieces of jewelry.

"I didn't know cowboys wore jewelry," Bert said in surprise.

Wes smiled. "The prizes are belt buckles or little ornaments of silver or gold which are worn on spur straps, hat bands, bridles—things like that," he explained. "The cowboys wear them when they compete in shows or dress up."

"That bad man who met us at the train had on a great big silver buckle," Flossie observed.

"Boots is different from most cowboys," Wes remarked. "He likes to show off all the time."

While the children had been talking, most of the rodeo winners had received their prizes. Now Bill Dayton walked up to the judges' stand.

"This fine silver and gold belt buckle to Mr. Bill Dayton for his spectacular riding!" the master of ceremonies cried.

"I hope it's prettier than the one Boots has," Flossie said.

"Come on," Nan urged. "Let's see if we can catch Bill. I want to ask him if he knows Bud Hixon."

Bert and Nan scurried through the departing crowd and made their way toward the area where the performers were gathered. They went from one cowboy to another inquiring for Bill Dayton, but no one had seen him.

"It looks as if we've missed him again," Nan said finally.

Disappointed, the twins gave up the search and hurried to join the others. On the way home Freddie announced that he was going to be a cowboy when he grew up.

"Oh, Freddie!" his twin teased. "I thought you wanted to be a fireman!"

"We—ll, I did, but now—" Freddie gazed wistfully at the many cowboys.

The next morning while the Bobbseys were at breakfast, Tom Yager came in and sat down beside Mrs. Bobbsey. He looked worried.

"One of the cowboys just rode in from the north range," he said. "He tells me at least ten head of cattle were stolen last night."

"Perhaps they've just strayed and the cowboys will be able to find them," Mrs. Bobbsey suggested.

Tom did not look hopeful. "It's difficult to trace cattle," he said. "You see, they all look more or less alike. So if the rustlers change the brands, it's almost impossible to recognize your own cattle."

"I can tell Star when I see her!" Freddie objected.

"That gives me an idea!" Bert cried. "Why not put Star out on one of the ranges? Then if she is stolen, you could spot her if you saw her on someone else's grazing land."

"And you could tell if the brand had been changed!" Nan put in.

"Say, Dad, that's a neat idea!" Wes exclaimed. "If we found Star with a strange brand on her, we could trace the brand and catch the thieves! You kids are good detectives!"

Deep in thought, the foreman got up and paced the floor for several minutes. Then he said, "It might work! I'll tell Johnny Bat to put Star and some other cattle in the north range. We'll see what happens!"

He left to give the necessary orders and a little later the twins looked out the window and saw two cowhands driving the cattle toward the north grazing area. Star frolicked up near the front of the group.

Freddie looked sadly at her. "I don't want Star to be stolen by those bad men!" he said.

"Cheer up! Don't lose hope!" Bert patted his small brother's shoulder. "Let's ride to the rodeo grounds and have a look at that covered wagon. Maybe we can find a clue while Nan and Flossie take their cooking lesson from Sing Foo."

The girls had already gone to the big ranch kitchen where the cook was beginning his preparations for dinner. He had measured the water and vinegar into a large pot and set it on the fire.

"What are you making?" Nan asked.

"Sucamagrowl," Sing Foo replied.

Flossie giggled. "Sookamagrowl, youkamagrowl!" she chanted. "That's a funny name,!"

Sing Foo tittered. "Very funny name, but very good chow!"

"What else do you put into it?" Nan asked when she saw the mixture boiling.

"You watch!" Sing Foo stirred some flour into two cups of sugar, then poured this into the boiling liquid. "Now we let cook fifteen minutes while make biscuit dough."

Quickly he put the shortening, flour, and baking powder together. He then broke off little pieces of the dough and began to drop them into the bubbling mixture.

"Let me!" Flossie pleaded. She climbed onto a chair and carefully let the dough balls fall into the pot.

"Look at them bounce around!" she cried in delight as the little dumplings began to cook in the simmering liquid.

Sing Foo brought out a bowl and set it on the table. "We put dumplings in this and keep hot in warming oven until dinner," he directed.

"Are they ready now?" Nan asked.

When the cook nodded, Nan picked up a ladle and carefully began to lift the dumplings from the pot to the bowl.

The girls and Sing Foo had been so absorbed in their cooking that they had not noticed Jenny, the pet hen, strolling in through the open door. She paraded around the kitchen, then hopped up onto the table.

Flossie heard a noise and turned around. She began to giggle. Jenny was wildly flapping her wings and trying to get rid of one of the dumplings which she held firmly in her beak. It was stuck fast.

Nan and Sing Foo turned to see what Flossie was laughing about. "Jenny's eating our sucamagrowl dessert!" Flossie cried. Then she realized the poor hen was in trouble.

"Jenny, very bad chicken!" Sing Foo scolded,

"Jenny, very bad chicken," Sing Foo scolded

taking the dumpling out of her mouth. Then
he shooed the pet off the table and out the door.

Meanwhile, Bert and Freddie had received
their parents' permission to go to town.

"You can't get lost just going there," Mrs.
Bobbsey said with a wink.

Their father added, "Don't go anywhere else."

The two boys promised, then ran to the corral. Bert saddled the horses and the brothers set off for Vinton. When they arrived at the rodeo grounds, they found the place deserted.

Bert tied the horses to the railing of a fence which encircled the grounds. Then they walked over to the covered wagon at the entrance. The old vehicle with its arched top of canvas stood by itself.

"Let's climb inside," Freddie suggested.

"Okay." Bert boosted his brother into the back of the old wagon, then climbed up himself. The inside was dusty and empty except for two long benches which ran down the sides.

"There's nothing here," Bert declared. "I had hoped we'd find something connected with that note you found in the cabin."

Freddie had spotted the high seat at the front of the vehicle. "I'm going to pretend I'm driving across the desert," he declared, scrambling up. "Giddyap!" the little boy called, cracking a make-believe whip.

Bert spotted a few pieces of paper under one of the benches. He got on his knees to examine them.

Freddie looked back, then climbed down to join his brother. "Did you find a clue?" he asked.

Bert did not reply. He was busy spreading out a paper which seemed to have been torn from a magazine.

In the silence both boys suddenly became aware of men's voices just outside. They looked at each other. Was this covered wagon the meeting place mentioned in the note?

Bert nudged Freddie to be quiet. The boys listened intently.

Two men were speaking in low tones, and it was impossible to hear their words. The conversation seemed to be a serious one. Finally one of the men raised his voice.

When Bert leaned forward to listen he glanced at Freddie. The little boy was making an agonized face, trying not to sneeze! Bert motioned for his brother to press a finger just above his upper lip, but it was too late!

Achoo! Freddie gave a terrific sneeze!

At once there was silence outside the covered wagon. Then a head appeared in the rear opening. It was that of the cowboy, Del Logan!

"Get out of there!" he shouted angrily.

CHAPTER VIII

SUGAR BABY

"WE'RE not hurting anything!" Freddie protested as the boys climbed out of the covered wagon.

Bert calmly asked the angry cowboy, "Were you looking for us?"

"Why—er—no," Del replied. "I had an errand to do in town and just happened to see this friend of mine. I stopped to talk to him."

Del turned to speak to his companion, but the man had quickly mounted his horse and ridden off.

Embarassed, Del blustered, "You kids better stay on the ranch where you belong. If you don't, you'll get into trouble! What were you doin' in that wagon anyway?"

Bert replied, "We've studied about them in school and we wanted to see one close up. Are there any other covered wagons around here?"

Del looked startled. "N-not that I remember," he said, "but the West is full of them.

As for this one, it's private property. Stay out of it!"

As the boys hesitated to leave, he thundered at them, "Get on your horses and go home!"

Del Logan waited until they had mounted and set off. Bert had a notion to go back and do some more searching. But the cowboy stayed there watching them, so at last Bert gave up and headed for the ranch.

"He acted awful funny," Freddie observed. "Why was he so mad at us for looking for clues?"

"I don't know," Bert said thoughtfully. "Maybe he was afraid we had heard what he and his friend were talking about."

A wild idea popped into Freddie's head. "Do you think Del is one of the rustlers, Bert?" he asked excitedly.

Bert stared at his little brother. "That might explain why he is so unfriendly. Anyhow, I think we should watch him carefully."

When they reached home, the boys told Nan and Flossie about Del. The girls agreed that the cowboy's actions were suspicious. "We'll watch him, too," Nan said.

Later at the dinner table, when the sucama-growl had been eaten and highly praised, Flossie spoke up. "I'd like to go see Mr. Kirby and thank him for sending Mr. Dawkins to rescue us."

"I think that's a very nice idea," Mrs. Bobbsey agreed. "Perhaps Wes knows how to get to the fire tower."

"Did you say *Mr.* Kirby?" Wes seemed surprised.

"Yes," said Flossie. "He lives on the top of a mountain!"

The ranch boy looked at his father with a grin. "Shall I take the twins to visit Kirby?" he asked.

"Sure," the foreman replied, his eyes twinkling.

It was decided that the twins would go with Wes the following day. The boy had some chores to take care of first but said he would be ready to leave directly after dinner.

The next morning while the children were playing in front of the ranch house, Johnny Bat rode in. "It looks like your plan might work, Bert," he called. "Ten of those cattle we drove up to the north pasture have disappeared!"

"Was Star with them?" Freddie asked quickly.

Johnny nodded grimly. "I'm goin' in the house now to notify the sheriff," he told them.

"I hope they find Star soon," Freddie said. "I don't want her to get too far away."

Immediately after the noon meal, the twins and Wes set out on horseback for the fire tower. Freddie was so excited he was bubbling over.

"I've decided for sure I'll be a fire watcher when I grow up!" he announced. "I'll bet Kirby is a great big man like this!" Freddie sat tall in the saddle and threw out his chest until the buttons on his shirt almost popped off.

"I thought you were going to be a cowboy," Bert teased his little brother. Flossie and Nan giggled.

Wes grinned but said nothing. The group rode across the green valley and started up into the hills. Here the going was rougher. A narrow trail wound up the mountainside. The rocky ground was dotted with clumps of sagebrush and occasional pine trees.

As they rounded a curve, Wes pointed up to the very top of the mountain. "There's the fire station." The children saw a small building perched on a very tall metal frame.

"It looks like a little birdhouse!" Nan exclaimed.

By now the trail had almost disappeared. Wes swung out of his saddle. "It's getting too steep for our mounts," he said. "We'll have to walk the rest of the way. Tie up the horses. You'll find hobbles in your saddlebags."

The twins pulled out the leather shackles that resembled straps and Wes showed them how to attach them to their animals' front legs.

"Now tie the reins to the hobble," he directed,

"and your horse will be here when you get back."

A few minutes later Wes and the twins began the scramble over the rocks toward the lookout tower. It was hard work, and everyone was panting when they arrived at the foot of the structure.

Looking up, they saw a small, square building of brown wood. A steep flight of steps at one side of the framework ran to the top.

"Goodness! What a lot of steps!" Nan observed.

Wes laughed. "It's a real climb."

With Flossie in the lead, the twins started up and Wes followed. "I'm going to count the steps," the little girl announced and began, "One, two, three—"

She had reached ten when suddenly something furry hit her shoulder. Flossie grabbed the rail to keep from falling.

"A kitty!" she cried. A little kitten had leaped onto her shoulder from the edge of the house porch. It clung there, purring contentedly.

"He's cute," Nan said.

The other children kept close behind Flossie as she continued climbing. In a few seconds they all stepped onto the platform surrounding the little building.

As Nan looked out over the country, she drew

in a deep breath. "What a wonderful view!" she cried. The whole valley and the bordering ranges of mountains were spread out before them.

Just then a door behind them opened and a soft voice said, "Good afternoon!"

The children whirled to see the speaker. There stood a plump little woman with short, curly white hair. She was smiling at them.

"Good afternoon, Kirby!" Wes said politely.

The twins stared in amazement. So this was Kirby, the fire watcher!

Grinning at their surprise, Wes introduced the Bobbseys and explained who they were. Mrs. Kirby welcomed them warmly.

"I see you've already made friends with Puffy," she said, taking the kitten from Flossie and cuddling it under her chin. "She keeps me company while I'm living at the tower. You see, I stay here from May to November all alone."

"I thought you would be a big man!" Freddie burst out. The woman laughed.

"You stay here all by yourself?" Nan asked.

"Yes. Come see my house."

The fire watcher led the children into a large room with windows all the way around. There was a gleaming white refrigerator and a stove on one side. In a corner stood a bed and next to it a low bookshelf. A table in the center of the room held a large disc about two feet across.

"What's that?" Freddie asked.

"My fire finder," Kirby explained. "I located your fire with this the other afternoon."

The woman showed the interested children how she could pinpoint the location of a fire by sighting through an instrument at the edge of the disc.

She also had binoculars. The twins took turns looking at the mountains through them. Freddie said under his breath, "I wish there'd be a fire!"

Mrs. Kirby had opened a cupboard under one of the windows. Now she brought out a big chocolate layer cake.

"This is my hobby," she said. "I love to make cake."

"It looks yummy!" said Nan.

Freddie asked, "Do you eat it all yourself?"

Kirby smiled. "Well, I hope to have nice people like you visit me; but when no one comes, I feed some of the cake to my animal friends."

She cut huge pieces for the children, and they munched happily. Wes was standing by the windows. Now he turned toward their hostess.

"Here comes one of your animal friends now, I think," he said.

"Who?"

"What?"

The twins crowded to the window and peered out. Trotting along among the rocks and trees was a little black bear! When he reached the base of the tower, he stopped. The bear sat back on his haunches and looked longingly up at the building.

"Isn't he sweet!" Flossie exclaimed.

Kirby laughed. "And he has a sweet tooth. That's why I call him Sugar Baby. Come outside," she added. "You can watch me feed him. Sugar is a regular visitor."

The children lined up along the rail. When the bear caught sight of them, he stood up on his hind legs and raised his snout into the air. Then he bounced up and down several times.

Freddie and Flossie squealed in delight. Kirby picked up the last slice of cake and gave it to Flossie to toss down to the bear.

"Here's your cake, Sugar Baby!" she said.

He caught it in his mouth and the cake disappeared in one gulp! Sugar stood there, looking hopefully at the balcony. Finally, when no more cake appeared, the bear turned and ambled off into the brush.

Freddie's interest returned to fires. "Where did you see our fire, Kirby?" he wanted to know.

The woman pointed toward the edge of the valley. "You see, I'm trained to keep looking out these windows all the time. Late last Monday afternoon I was standing at this window when I saw a wisp of black smoke. I couldn't imagine

The bear sat back on his haunches and looked up longingly

what it was since I knew no one lived down there any more."

"What did you do then?" Flossie asked eagerly.

"I used my finder and figured out just about where the fire was. Then I got Dawkins on the short-wave radio and asked him to go find out what was causing the smoke."

"And he found us!" Nan cried.

"I want to see Sugar Baby," Freddie said.

The little boy picked up the binoculars and focused them on the path the bear had taken.

"Do you see him?" Flossie asked. "Let me look!"

Freddie was about to hand the glasses to his twin when suddenly he stiffened. "I see Star!" he cried.

CHAPTER IX

CABIN CLUES

"STAR!" Flossie repeated. She took the glasses from Freddie and turned them in the direction he pointed. A second later she squealed, "I see her too! And lots of other cows!"

One after another the twins peered through the binoculars. Bert was last. "It *is* Star!" he declared. "Let's go over there! We can see if the brand on her has been changed."

Wes explained the situation to Kirby and asked if she could tell them how to reach the distant mountainside.

The children watched breathlessly while the woman lined up the instrument on the fire finder with the place where they had seen the calf. In a few minutes, she gave Wes directions.

"Ride due north for about five miles. You'll have to cross a couple of gullies, but you should be able to find the place."

The children thanked the fire watcher and

climbed down from the tower. They scrambled down the mountain to the trail where they had left their horses. Everyone mounted, then started off with Wes in the lead.

The ground was even rougher here, and the riders were forced to travel slowly. Wes picked the easiest way, but they still had to go up and down and around the mountains.

"Are you sure we're going in the right direction?" Nan finally asked when they had ridden almost an hour.

"I'm keeping the sun to our left," Wes replied. "We're going north, but if we don't find the cattle pretty soon, we'll have to turn toward home."

The searchers rode on in silence for several minutes until they reached a more open, smooth area. Wes speeded up. "There are some cattle on that hillside ahead! Maybe they're the ones we're looking for."

Freddie caught up to Wes. He peered eagerly at the animals. As they drew nearer, the little boy stood up in his stirrups and pointed. "There's Star! I know it is!"

The brown-and-white calf was on the far side of the grazing area. Freddie pulled his whistle from his pocket and made a gentle sound with it.

The calf raised her head, then began to trot toward the children. They all dismounted and, leading their horses, walked over to the grazing cattle. Wes put his hand on Star's rump and carefully examined the brand mark.

"It's been changed from the original one," he said excitedly.

The Bobbseys gathered around, and the boy showed them the brand. It was a circle with a bar in the center.

"Are the other cattle branded the same way?" Nan asked.

Wes walked among the animals, who were nudging him curiously. Many of them bore the same circle and bar mark, he said.

"Do you think they're the ones Johnny Bat put in the north range yesterday?" Bert questioned.

"They could be," Wes replied.

"Then I have a clue to the rustlers," Bert said, remembering the branding iron he had found in the deserted cabin. It had been a circle and bar. He quickly told Wes about the twins' visit to the shabby dwelling and the things they had seen there.

Wes was excited. "It would be easy to put a brand like that over our half circle! And these brands all look fresh! Say, do you think you could find that cabin again?"

Bert and Nan consulted each other, then Bert said, "It may not be far from here—down the mountain, just before you reach the valley."

The Bobbseys gathered around, and the boy showed them
the brand

"Let's go!" Wes cried. "Maybe we can catch
those thieves!"

"Don't you think we ought to call the
sheriff?" Nan suggested.

"I will as soon as we get home," Wes agreed.
"If we can find out more about this cabin, it
might be helpful to him."

Freddie did not want to leave Star, but the others assured him the calf would be safe. Reluctantly, Freddie mounted his pony.

"Be careful going downhill," Wes cautioned. "Don't let your horse step in a hole."

The group set off, cautiously holding their horses in check. Suddenly Nan reined in.

"Wait a minute! I see something!" she called to the others.

Nan slipped from her saddle and picked up a shiny object from the dirt. It was a silver belt buckle.

Flossie and the boys gathered around as she turned it over in her hand. When the dust had been brushed off, they saw that the buckle had a very elaborate design on it. There was a rectangle with a carving around the edge and in the center a steer head of gold with ruby eyes.

"Wow!" exclaimed Wes. "Some buckle!"

"Do you think it's the prize Bill Dayton won at the rodeo?" Nan asked.

Bert looked worried. "If it is, Bill might be one of the rustlers!" he declared.

Wes was indignant. "I never saw such a fancy buckle given at a rodeo," he said. "Besides, I'm sure Bill has nothing to do with the rustlers. He's a good guy!"

Nan sighed. "Anyway, I wish we could talk to him," she said. "We want to ask him about Bud Hixon."

A sudden thought struck Bert. *"Say!"* he exclaimed. "Maybe this buckle belongs to Boots. *He* likes to wear fancy things."

The others agreed, but Wes was impatient to go on to the cabin. "Perhaps we'll find more clues there," he said.

The riders pressed forward until Flossie pulled up beside Nan. "I'm awful thirsty," she said. "I wish we could find a drinking fountain!"

Wes heard her and laughed. "I'm afraid we don't have any fountains around, but we have something better—a mountain stream! Come on!"

He branched off the trail toward a spot where a stream came bubbling down from the mountain. It was bordered by high grass and a few rocks.

"Watch out for snakes!" Wes cautioned as the twins dismounted.

"Snakes!" Nan looked nervous. "How do you watch out for snakes?"

"Like this." Wes cut several small branches from a nearby sapling. "Swish one of these in front of you as you walk. That will make the snakes leave if there are any about."

The four Bobbseys, pushing the sticks in front of them, advanced toward the stream. When they reached the water, the twins knelt down and flattened themselves on their stomachs.

They drank the clear cold water as it passed over the rocks.

"Ooh, it tastes good!" Flossie cried, raising her dripping face and grinning at Freddie.

Feeling refreshed, the children made their way back to the spot where they had left the horses. As they approached, Flossie's Indian pony pulled loose from the small tree to which he had been tied. The next moment he went galloping off!

"My horse!" Flossie screamed. "Somebody catch him!"

With a running jump Wes landed in his saddle. He took off at full speed after the fleeing pony. The twins watched breathlessly as Wes pulled up to Flossie's horse. They saw him lean over, grasp the flying reins, and bring the pony to a halt.

A few minutes later he led the runaway back to the group. "I'm afraid the pony wasn't tied very well, Flossie," Wes said. "That's one thing you must make sure of out here. A cowboy without his horse is pretty helpless."

Flossie promised to be more careful in the future. They all mounted and rode on toward the cabin.

The sun was hanging low in the sky by the time Bert spied the little building through the trees. It appeared to be empty.

Nan reined in her horse. "Why don't you boys

see if anyone is inside?" she suggested. "I'll wait here with Freddie and Flossie."

Bert and Wes tied their horses and walked toward the cabin. Wes knocked on the door. There was no answer.

"I guess no one's here," he said. "I'm going in."

Bert waved to Nan while Wes pushed open the door and entered the cabin. Bert said, "Everybody seems to leave doors unlocked around here."

The cowboy chuckled. "Right. It's the custom out West."

Nan and the younger twins tied their horses and ran up. They followed the boys into the one-room shack. Nan hurried to the table where the map had been.

It was gone! The branding iron, too, had disappeared.

"Well, someone's been here since Wednesday, that's for sure!" Bert declared. "Let's see if we can find a clue as to who he was."

The children poked around the littered room looking for anything which might shed light on the mystery of the cattle rustlers.

Flossie picked up a leather case with a flap pocket. "What's this?" she asked.

Wes came over to her and took the case. "It's a staple pocket," he explained. "It's used to carry wire staples when 'riding fence' and it's attached to the front or back saddle string."

He opened the case. A few staples fell out into his hand.

Bert had been examining some articles on a low shelf. "Here's a pair of pliers," he said. Wes was excited. "You know, we told you that the cattle were disappearing from the fenced-in ranges," he began.

The Bobbseys nodded.

"Well, these tools, the pliers and staples, that is, could be used for cutting—and mending—fences."

"You mean the thieves open the fences, drive the cattle out, then repair the fences?" Bert asked.

"Yes. I'd sure like to find out who owns this cabin!"

Bert picked up the pliers again and examined them. Then he whistled.

"Look!" he cried. "The Half Circle brand is marked on these pliers!"

CHAPTER X

A FOXY CUSTOM

"HALF Circle pliers!" Wes exclaimed. "That's queer!"

"Do you think whoever lives here took them from the ranch?" Nan suggested.

"It looks that way," Wes agreed. He examined the other tools in the cabin, but none bore the Half Circle mark.

"That's something else to tell the sheriff," Bert said.

A few minutes later the children left the cabin and mounted their horses. The sun was setting behind the mountains, and the valley was growing dark by the time the five riders reached level ground.

"It's too late for the sheriff to find the cabin tonight," Wes declared, "but I'll phone him when we get home."

When they arrived at the ranch, Wes went straight to the telephone. Meanwhile, Sing Foo put supper on the table. Mr. Bobbsey's eyes twinkled as the twins slipped into their places.

"I can see from your faces you've had an exciting day," he said. "I understand from Tom that Kirby is an unusual fire watcher!"

Flossie giggled. "She's a chocolate cake lady!"

Freddie could wait no longer to tell of their discoveries. "Guess what!" he burst out. "We found Star! And some other cattle!"

The grownups were amazed and asked for details. As the twins finished their story, Wes came in and said he could get no response from the sheriff's office. "I'll try later," he said.

Mr. Yager turned to Bert. "Your scheme worked perfectly!" he praised the boy. "You say the brand *has* been changed, Wes?" he asked his son.

Wes nodded and told about the circle-and-bar brand. "I'm sure the other cattle we saw are from this ranch too."

"Sheriff Werner can check the brand for us," Tom told Mrs. Bobbsey. He explained that under range laws all cattle brands had to be registered in the owner's name.

Mrs. Bobbsey said, "We're going into town to church tomorrow morning. If we can't get the sheriff on the phone, perhaps Wes and the twins can drive in earlier and see him."

The boys now described the articles they had

found in the cabin at the edge of the gully.

Tom looked worried. "It does sound as if that cabin might be the rustlers' hideout, but I can't understand how a pair of Half Circle pliers got there! You boys had better tell Johnny Bat about it. He's in charge of the fences."

"Speaking of Johnny," Mrs. Bobbsey spoke up, "he was here to give us an invitation. His niece Rainbow and his nephew River Deer want us to come to their reservation tomorrow afternoon. Something special is going on."

"Yippee!" cried Freddie and pranced around the room in his favorite war whoop dance.

The other children immediately tried to guess what the special event would be and even asked Tom Yager. He merely smiled and would not answer.

"Oh, you know what it is," Nan said. "You just won't tell."

"Guess you're right," Tom said calmly.

The next morning Bert went out directly after breakfast to find Johnny Bat. But the cowboy had ridden out earlier than usual to the range, so Bert was not able to inquire about the pliers.

Wes had no luck in contacting the sheriff, so the twins piled into one of the ranch cars, and Wes headed toward Vinton. It was decided that only he and Bert would call on the sheriff. Nan and the small twins would wait for them at The Frontier House.

When Wes had let Nan, Freddie, and Flossie out in front of the hotel, Flossie took Nan's hand. "I'm thirsty," she announced, "and hungry. I'd like a strawberry soda!"

"Me too!" Freddie said immediately.

Nan looked around. "I guess we could go in that room where we had supper the first night. They probably have sodas."

The dining room was empty except for four men seated at a table. They were deep in conversation. One was lean and wore an elaborate cowboy outfit.

Freddie stared over at him, then whispered, "There's Boots! I'm going to ask him why he left us at that old house!" The little boy started across the room.

At the sound of Freddie's voice the cowboy had looked up. He spoke in a low tone to his companions. Quickly they all arose and hurried from the dining room.

Freddie turned back to his sisters. "Why did Boots run away?" he asked in surprise.

"I guess he didn't want to talk to you," Nan replied. "Probably he feels guilty."

Suddenly she noticed the diorama of the covered wagon which the children had seen when they had been in the dining room before. An idea flashed through Nan's mind. Could *this* be the covered wagon referred to in the note the children had found in the cabin?

Then the girl thought of the fancy silver buckle, and Bert's suspicion that it might belong to Boots. Was the cowboy connected with the cabin and the branding iron?

Nan and the twins had finished their sodas and were waiting on the porch of the hotel when the boys arrived. Fortunately they had found Sheriff Werner.

"We told him about seeing Star and the things we found in that cabin," Bert reported. "He's going to check on the circle-and-bar brand tomorrow morning and let us know who uses it."

"Is he going to get Star?" Freddie asked anxiously.

"Yes. One of his deputies will meet Johnny Bat tomorrow," Wes said. "They'll drive the cattle back to our range."

As he and the children walked toward the church where they were to meet Mr. and Mrs. Bobbsey, Nan told the boys about Boots and his hurried departure.

"Do you think that covered wagon in the diorama could be the one mentioned in the note?" she asked.

"Say, maybe it is!" Bert cried.

Wes laughed. "You'll have a hard time deciding which is the right covered wagon," he said. "As you know, these wagons are all over the West."

"Why did Boots run away?" Freddie asked in surprise

When the church service was over the Bobbseys went to The Frontier House to have midday dinner. Wes returned to the ranch.

"I wish I knew what the s'prise is at the
Indian village," Flossie said. "Then I could eat
my dinner better."

The others laughed. "You won't have long to
wait," her mother said.

Promptly at three o'clock the visitors arrived
at the reservation. Rainbow and River Deer met
them at a gateway entrance. The visitors were
fascinated by the sight before them. The grassy
area was dotted with reddish tan houses, some
four stories high.

"Indian make house out of mud and straw
bricks," River Deer explained. "We call
adobe."

"Oh, see the little round buildings in front of
them!" Nan said. "Are they the places where
you bake your bread?"

"Yes," Rainbow answered. "And Indian
grow own wheat and corn to make bread."

Most of the men wore American style clothes,
but the women had on rather long black dresses,
wrapped over one shoulder and belted at the
waist. Moccasins and shawls or blankets com-
pleted their costumes.

"Aren't those blankets colorful?" Mrs. Bobbsey remarked. "If any are for sale, I'd like to
buy one."

"My mommy sell blankets," said Rainbow. "Come! I show you."

As she led the way through the village, Bert noticed a mountain in the background. The upper part of the steep slope was dotted with caves reached by a long, narrow ladder. Mr. Bobbsey said these had been the homes of the Indians who had lived there many, many years ago.

"They were called cliff dwellers," he added.

"I want to see them," Freddie announced.

River Deer grinned. "After ceremony you see. White man call them first American apartment house."

The Bobbseys smiled. By now they had reached the Indian children's house. Their parents stood outside smiling. Johnny Bat's sister looked very much like him, but was stout. The father was tall and slender.

Rainbow introduced the visitors. She surprised the twins by giving their play Indian names.

"This Chief Roman Nose Bert," she said. "Big girl Singing Brook. Little girl Jumping Rabbit. Her twin Little Wolf."

"Rainbow, you're wonderful to remember," Nan praised her. "Johnny Bat must have told you."

River Deer now turned to his mother and spoke to her in Tiwa, the language of the Pueblo

Indians. The woman beckoned the visitors to follow her inside the main room of the house. The walls and floor were covered with rugs.

"Oh, how bee-yoo-ti-ful!" Flossie cried out.

Rainbow's mother spoke to her children in Tiwa. Then River Deer pointed to a fine red, white, and black rug hanging near a small fireplace in which lay piñon wood ready to light.

"You like this rug?" the Indian boy asked Mrs. Bobbsey.

"Oh, yes, very much," she replied.

"My mother say she give it to you because you nice friend."

At once Mr. Bobbsey spoke up. "Oh, thank you, but we could not accept such a valuable gift."

Johnny's relatives looked hurt and Nan whispered to her father, "I've read that you must never refuse a gift an Indian offers."

"I see." Mr. Bobbsey turned to River Deer. "Please tell us what your custom is."

The Indian boy grinned. "Custom is you give present too."

"But I have nothing with me but money," the twins' father said.

"Money be fine gift," River Deer replied.

At this everyone burst into laughter, and Mr. Bobbsey said, "Pretty foxy! I can't buy the rug. But you give it to me and I give you money!"

Just then a drum sounded in the distance.

"Come on!" Freddie exclaimed. "There's going to be a war!"

"Hold on!" said Mr. Bobbsey, and Freddie halted. "The Indians will lead the way to the surprise."

Before they started off, the Indian children and their father put on feathered headdresses. Then they found extra ones for the twins, who marched along proudly.

The surprise was a ceremony which was to take place at the far end of the village. As the Bobbseys neared it with the Indians, they could see a great crowd assembling around a very tall pole. Tied by its feet to the top was a small eagle. Every few moments it would flap its beautiful wings and scream in anger.

River Deer now explained that the boys of the tribe were about to play a game. Taking turns, they would climb the pole and try to bring the eagle to the ground without being injured by the bird's beak.

"Boy who get eagle keep feathers for new hat," River Deer said.

"Oh, it looks dangerous!" Nan exclaimed. She also thought the idea of pulling out the eagle's feathers was cruel but said nothing.

When everyone in the village had assembled, the chief, wearing a long and beautiful feathered headdress, made a speech in Tiwa. River Deer turned excitedly to Bert.

"He say you try to get eagle like Indian boys. Watch me and two others, then you climb. Man beat drum when time up."

Bert's heart began to pound as he nodded. He could not refuse and be a coward in front of the whole tribe!

The three Indians each climbed the pole easily, but the eagle put up such a fight that they were not able to loosen the bird without danger of its pecking at them and causing real injury. The drum had sounded three times and each boy had been forced to slide down.

Now it was Bert Bobbsey's turn! Drawing on all his courage, he stepped forward and began to shin up the pole!

CHAPTER XI

ANGRY EAGLE

BERT'S family held their breath as he began his climb up the pole. Halfway to the top he paused as the eagle gave a piercing cry and banged its wings in panic against the wood.

"Do I dare try it?" Bert wondered, almost giving up.

As the bird quieted down, the boy took heart and shinned up the rest of the way. He murmured soothingly to the eagle, "I won't hurt you. What's losing a few feathers mean to you?"

Bert shielded his face with one arm, while he tried to untie the thong that held the bird to the pole. The eagle, apparently tired from struggling, made no move to harm the boy.

"I've almost got it loose," he said.

Those on the ground were amazed at what was happening. Was this white boy from Lakeport going to walk off with the honors?

Suddenly the thong came loose. Before Bert

could grab the bird's feet, it gave a tremendous pull. The tied legs shed their binding. The next instant the eagle was free!

"Oh!" Bert cried out.

The Indians gasped in dismay. Their prize was gone! They began to murmur among themselves. Some looked accusingly at the chief as if he were to blame because he had let Bert enter the contest.

The Bobbseys were sorry for Bert's predicament, but when Nan said, "I'm glad the poor bird got free," they all nodded.

Bert took a deep breath, then slid to the ground. He walked directly to the chief and said, "I'm very sorry, sir."

The chief spoke in Tiwa, and River Deer translated. "He say your courage great. Forget mistake. Indian boys play different game."

Bert's family knew how embarrassed he was, and Mr. Bobbsey suggested that they should now return to the ranch.

"We'll go back to Rainbow's house first and pick up the rug."

The two Indian children accompanied them. On the way Nan's mind turned to the two mysteries the twins were trying to solve. On a chance, she asked, "Rainbow and River Deer, have you ever heard of a man named Bud Hixon?"

Surprised, the boy said, "Yes, Singing Brook.

He come here many time. You know him?"

Nan explained about Bud's father. "Where can we find Bud?" she asked eagerly.

"I not know. Hixon come here once in a while. Not see him in long time."

The Bobbseys were excited. Now at last they had a clue to the missing man!

"If he visits you again," Nan said, "please tell him to come to the Half Circle Ranch. It's very important."

The twins and their parents thanked the Indians for their hospitality, picked up the rug, and set off for the ranch. As soon as they reached it, the children ran to the bunkhouse to find Johnny Bat and tell him about their visit to the reservation.

Their friend was seated in the doorway strumming a guitar. "How is Chief Roman Nose?" he called to Bert as the children came up. "Did you get the eagle feathers?"

"Oh, so you knew what the surprise was?" Bert said and told Johnny the sad story. The Indian merely laughed. "That happens sometimes."

Flossie spoke up. "Now we have lots to tell our teacher about Indians," she said.

"Yes," Nan agreed. "I'm going to start tonight writing my paper."

"Johnny," said Bert, "have you missed any pliers lately?"

"Pliers?" Johnny repeated. "Son, we've got so many pliers around here I could never tell if a pair was missin' or not."

Bert told him about the pair which the children had found in the cabin. "It had the Half Circle mark on it," he said.

Suddenly an angry voice came from inside the bunkhouse. "What were you kids doin' snoopin' around people's cabins?"

The next moment Del Logan appeared in the doorway. He leaned against the side and scowled at the children.

"We weren't snooping!" Bert replied hotly. "We're trying to find the rustlers who've been stealing our cattle."

"Cowboys lose pliers all the time," Del remarked. "Anyone could pick them up."

He turned to go back into the bunkhouse but paused for a parting shot. "You'll have to find somethin' more important than pliers," he sneered, "if you're goin' to catch the rustlers."

Johnny began to strum a tune. "Don't mind Del," he said. "You're smart kids. Maybe you *can* find these cattle thieves!"

Just then Sing Foo rang the bell for supper. The twins said good-by to Johnny and went to the house. After a delicious roast beef meal, Bert and Nan took notebooks out under a tree in front of the house to start writing about the Indian reservation.

Freddie and Flossie wandered off to the chicken yard to visit Jenny, Sing Foo's pet hen. The cook had gathered a basket of eggs and left them on a shelf which jutted out from the side of the henhouse.

"I guess Sing Foo forgot his eggs," Flossie observed. "Let's take them to the kitchen."

As she started to pick up the basket, the twins heard a *cluck, cluck* from the roof of the house. They looked up to see Jenny pacing back and forth.

"She can't get down!" Freddie cried. "I'll help her!"

He looked about for something to stand on. Several egg crates were piled nearby. Quickly Freddie pulled the crates over to the wall of the chicken house and began to climb up on them.

"Be careful, Freddie!" Flossie warned as the crates swayed perilously.

Freddie reached the top crate and stretched out his hand to grab Jenny. But the hen jumped back out of reach. As Freddie leaned farther forward, the crates suddenly collapsed!

Grabbing wildly for something to stop his fall, the little boy's hand hit the basket of eggs. Freddie landed on the ground, the eggs on top of him! He struggled to his feet, dripping egg yolks!

Jenny flew down from the roof and stalked away, clucking disapprovingly. "Jenny!" Freddie cried. "You could get down all by your-self!"

Flossie giggled. "Oh, Freddie, you look such a mess!"

At that moment Sing Foo came to get his eggs. When he saw Freddie, he stopped short and threw his hands in the air. "What happen?"

"He didn't mean to break your eggs," Flossie cried. "He just wanted to help Jenny get down from the roof."

"No matter," the cook said, shaking with laughter. "Jenny very bad chicken. You come in kitchen, Freddie. Sing Foo wash you!"

Next morning the children waited anxiously for the sheriff to telephone. When he did, Wes took the call. A surprised look came over the boy's face as he listened.

"That circle and bar brand isn't registered!" Wes reported to the twins as he turned from the telephone. "Also, the sheriff says he sent a deputy to that field early this morning and there were no cattle in it."

"Star's gone again!" Freddie wailed. "And you said she'd be all right!"

"Don't worry," Nan said, rumpling her little brother's hair. "We'll find Star."

The children, together with several cowboys, made a wide search that day. They found no

Freddie's hand hit the basket of eggs

clue to Star or the other cattle. By bedtime they were all discouraged.

Bert, worried, lay awake for some time, then fell asleep. He was awakened suddenly by a strange sound. Bert looked over at Freddie, but the little boy was sleeping peacefully.

The sound came again. *Whoooo!*

"That's funny," Bert thought. "It must be an owl, but I haven't heard any here before. Maybe it's in that tree just outside."

Silently he slipped out of bed and tiptoed to the window which overlooked the rear yard and the cowboys' bunkhouse. There was no moon, but the sky was full of stars.

Bert was peering up into the tree when his attention was caught by a moving figure. Coming from the bunkhouse was the shadowy form of a man. A coil of rope swung from his right arm.

"Who's that?" Bert wondered. As he leaned for a better look, the man disappeared into the darkness.

CHAPTER XII

TRAILING THIEVES

"WHAT's going on?" Bert asked himself, mystified. "I wonder if that man is stealing something!" Hurriedly he put on slippers and robe and ran outside.

Bert walked around the bunkhouse, peering into the shadows, but he saw no one. Everything was still. "Maybe it was just one of the cowboys," he decided and went back to bed.

The next morning when he and Freddie reached the breakfast table they found Tom Yager talking seriously to their parents.

"Good morning, boys," Mrs. Bobbsey said. "Tom has bad news. Johnny Bat has just come in from the south range. More cattle have been stolen!"

In the excitement which followed, Nan said, "Let's ride out there and look for clues!"

Wes was free that morning and agreed to take the older twins. Freddie and Flossie were to receive a riding lesson from Johnny Bat.

"Try to stay on your horse!" Bert teased.

Wes started off with Bert and Nan across the valley at an easy canter. After an hour's ride, they reached the edge of the south range. Though some cattle were grazing, it was evident that many were missing.

The three riders went along the fence slowly, studying the ground for anything which would give them a clue to the rustlers.

Finally at the far side, away from the ranch, Bert pulled up. "Do you think these horses' tracks mean anything, Wes?" he asked.

The ground at this point was churned up with prints on both sides of the fence.

Wes dismounted and examined the wire. "I think it's been cut here and then mended!"

"Then maybe," Nan cried, "that's how the staples and pliers were used!"

"Let's follow the tracks!" Bert proposed.

The three riders moved at a slow pace, examining the prints.

"Two horses were here," Wes observed, "one on either side of the cattle."

Bert nodded. "It looks as if the men were driving the herd alone."

"This is odd!" Nan exclaimed suddenly and rode off a distance to the right of the jumble of prints. "Another set of tracks!"

Her brother guided his horse to the place where Nan was pointing. "A third man!" he declared. "Perhaps he was acting as a lookout to warn the rustlers if anyone approached."

"Could be—if he was with the rustlers," Wes said. "It's possible though, that he came along afterward. He may have followed the rustlers' tracks just as we are doing now."

Bert nodded. "Or maybe he was watching the thieves, keeping a little distance behind them."

The trail gradually led the children up into the mountains. Here the ground was rocky and uneven, and the tracks were harder to follow.

Bert rode in the lead. They were proceeding beside the edge of a gully when suddenly he reined in. "It looks as if a horse slipped and fell over here," he declared.

Wes and Nan hurried up beside him. From the path down toward the bottom of the gully there was a wide trail of broken bushes.

"Maybe someone is hurt!" Nan exclaimed.

Wes and the twins quickly dismounted and hobbled their horses. Then they carefully made their way down the steep slope. Bert was first to reach the floor of the gully.

"I don't see anybody," he called back to Wes and Nan. "The horse must have been able to get up and walk away."

The three examined the ground where the animal had evidently struggled to its feet. Nan picked up something from under a bush. It was a red silk scarf.

"Look!" she cried. "The rider must have dropped this!"

Wes took the kerchief. "This is like Bill Dayton's." He showed her the print of tiny horses with which the silk was ornamented.

"What would Bill have been doing here?" Bert asked.

Wes shrugged. "I don't know. But we'd better follow those tracks for a while. He may have been hurt in that fall." Wes pointed out the uneven horseshoe marks. "The horse was limping," he said.

The searchers went on for some distance, until the prints disappeared at the bank of a little stream.

"We'll have to go back for our horses," Wes said. "We can't go any farther. I guess if Bill had been hurt, we'd have found him by now."

The three turned and began to retrace their steps. Suddenly Nan stopped. "Listen!" she said.

As the three stood quietly they heard a horse whinny.

"He's near here," Wes cried. "Come on!"

Once more the children made their way along the stream. Finally they saw the horse standing in a clump of cottonwood trees on the far side of the brook.

"That's Bill's horse all right," Wes declared, noting the heavy black-and-white coat markings. "But where is Bill?"

At this spot the stream was shallow, and several flat rocks rose above the surface. Bert and Nan followed Wes across it on natural steppingstones. The horse whinnied a welcome.

"He's in pretty bad shape," Wes observed, pointing to the scratches and cuts on the animal's side and one leg.

"Can we get him to the ranch?" Nan asked, feeling sorry for the injured horse.

"I think so," Wes replied. "I'll lead him and we'll take it slow."

"Before we start back," said Nan, "let's search farther in case Bill Dayton's nearby." They climbed up the far side of the gully and peered among the rocks. There was no sign of the cowboy.

"Looks as if we'll have to give up," Wes decided.

Reluctantly, the twins agreed. Both were disappointed at not finding Bill. Also, they were worried. What could have happened to him?

Wes and Bert turned toward the stream. Nan hurried to follow. But as she walked along the edge of the bank, the soft earth gave way beneath her. The next instant she was sliding down the steep slope!

"Help!" Nan screamed.

"Grab something!" Bert yelled to his twin.

There was nothing to grab, however, and Nan

landed in the creek with a splash! Bert slid down and pulled her out of the water.

"Are you hurt?" he asked anxiously.

Nan walked a few steps. "I think I've twisted my ankle," she said, wincing. "And am I wet!"

"The sun will soon dry you off," Wes told her with a grin. "And Bert and I can carry you."

"But you have to lead Bill's horse!" Nan protested.

"Don't worry. I'll manage you both!"

Wes looped the horse's reins around his arm, then grasped Bert's wrists to form a seat for Nan. They struggled on this way until she declared she felt able to walk.

With both Nan and the horse limping, the group made their way back to where they had left their own mounts. Before starting for the ranch, the three searchers ate the sandwiches which Sing Foo had tucked into their saddlebags. Wes, leading the crippled horse behind him, made the trip home slowly. It was late afternoon by the time the tired riders came to the corral.

Sing Foo was standing by the fence talking to Johnny Bat. When he saw the injured horse, he ran over and took the reins.

"Sing Foo good horse doctor!" he chuckled. "You leave him to me. Fix him up good as new!"

Wes's father and Mr. and Mrs. Bobbsey

"Are you hurt, Nan?" Bert asked anxiously

joined the group and listened with interest to the children's tale of trying to track the stolen cattle.

"Now we know how the rustlers get the cattle out of the field," Tom mused. "But I wonder what Bill Dayton was doing around there."

"Maybe we can take his horse to him tomorrow and find out," Wes suggested. "That is, if he's back at the cabin."

Sing Foo led the animal into the stable and gently washed the cuts and scratches. Next he applied disinfectant to the wounds, then dusted healing powder over them.

He straightened up when the children entered. "After good dinner and night's rest, horse feel better," Sing Foo declared.

Wes, Bert, and Nan returned to the corral. Freddie and Flossie came running up. "I'm glad you're back," Freddie panted. "Johnny is going to show us how he puts on a roping act at the rodeo. We've been waiting for you."

"Okay, let's go!" Bert said. The twins and Wes moved into the yard, and the cowboy brought out his rope. They sat on the grass and the show began.

Holding the coil of rope in his left hand, Johnny twirled the loop over his head horizontally, then vertically at his side. He explained that different methods are used to catch a horse or steer by the head or feet. Next, he twirled the rope into a loop on the ground and stepped in and out of it.

The children applauded loudly, and Johnny grinned. "I could do a lot better," he said, "but my trick rope was taken from the nail in the bunkhouse last night. I guess someone borrowed it."

He explained that ropes were made of various materials. His favorite exhibition rope was braided cotton, while the one he had been using was ordinary Manila hemp.

A startling thought came to Bert. Had the mysterious man he had seen the previous night stolen Johnny's rope? But why?

Bert told the cowboy the incident. Johnny did not seem disturbed.

"There are people walking in and out of that bunkhouse all the time," he said. "Nobody would take my rope on purpose. It'll turn up!"

After Johnny had gone back to his work, Del Logan strolled over to the children. "You want to ride a real cowboy horse?" he asked Bert.

"Sure."

None of the other cowboys was around when Del led the children to the corral. He brought a gray horse from the stable.

The animal seemed to be nervous, jerking his head up and down and prancing sideways.

"Be careful, Bert," Nan said nervously. "That horse looks mean!"

"Don't get on if you're scared," Del said with a sneer. "I thought you wanted to learn how to ride rodeo style."

"I'm not scared," Bert declared. While Del held the horse, he swung into the saddle.

The animal stood quiet for a second. Suddenly he put his head down and bucked. Taken unawares, Bert clutched the saddle horn. He clung to it until he regained his balance.

Twisting, turning and leaping, the bronc went around the corral. Bert stuck tight. Then came a particularly vicious buck.

The boy flew from the saddle!

CHAPTER XIII

FRONTIER DAYS

"BERT!" screamed Nan. She ran toward her twin, who lay motionless on the ground. Del Logan had disappeared. Flossie and Freddie raced into the house for help.

As Nan reached Bert, he sat up and shook his head dizzily. A minute later he struggled to his feet.

"I'm all right," he declared. "Just had the wind knocked out of me!"

Flossie and Freddie came back with Tom Yager. The foreman was relieved to see Bert on his feet.

When Nan told what had happened, Tom's face turned red with anger. "You say it was Del?" he stormed. "He knows that horse isn't safe to ride!"

By morning Bert felt fine. He and Nan ran out to the stable to see Bill's horse. It whinnied in a friendly way as they walked up to the stall.

The animal seemed to have recovered completely.

"Maybe we can take him back to Bill," Nan suggested. "Then we'd have a chance to ask him about Bud Hixon."

Wes was willing to go with them, but Freddie and Flossie chose to stay at the ranch. Sing Foo had promised to teach them a Chinese game.

Before the older children started out, Wes phoned the sheriff and gave him a full account of their discovery the day before. At once he, too, became worried about Bill Dayton.

"If Bill was trailing those rustlers," Sheriff Werner said, "he may be in trouble. Sure is strange he'd leave his horse. I'll see what I can find out and let you know."

Once more Bert, Nan, and Wes rode across the green valley and up into the mountains.

As they drew near the cabin Nan spoke up. "I hope Bill's here today. We haven't much time left at the ranch to find out anything about Mr. Hixon's son."

"Or to catch the rustlers," Bert added.

"Hi, Bill!" Wes shouted. The three dismounted and walked toward the little dwelling.

The door was closed. Wes knocked. There was no reply, but a strange noise met their ears. It sounded as if someone were dragging a heavy object across the floor.

"Maybe he's hurt and can't answer!" Nan cried.

She pulled the door open. At once they saw the big black dog standing in the middle of the room. A boot was hanging from his mouth.

When he caught sight of the visitors, he dropped the boot and bounded toward them. Going from one child to another, he placed his front paws on their shoulders and licked their cheeks!

This time Bert noticed a collar on the dog's neck. He pulled it around and read the name Cinder engraved on the plate.

"Hi there, Cinder!" Bert said, patting the huge animal on the head. "You're some 'fierce dog'!"

"He was dragging the boot," Nan remarked. "That's the strange noise we heard."

"Where's Bill, Cinder?" Wes asked.

The dog looked beseechingly at the boy. Then Cinder wagged his tail and whined. The children glanced around the cabin. The cot did not look as if it had been slept in, and the dog's bowl was empty.

"I think Cinder is hungry," Nan said. She got a box of dog biscuits from a shelf and gave several to the dog. He gulped them down quickly.

"I'll put the horse in the shelter, give Cinder water, and leave a note," Wes decided. "If we don't hear anything from Bill, we can come back tomorrow and feed the dog and the horse."

After doing this, he and the children mounted and rode off. They had not gone far before Bert heard a slight noise. He turned around to see Cinder following them.

"Go back!" Bert said sternly.

The dog stopped for a moment then trotted on after the riders. He continued to follow, despite repeated commands for him to go back.

Bert grinned. "We may as well let him come," he said.

Meanwhile, the younger twins had started to play a game with Sing Foo on the patio. "It's like dominoes!" Flossie exclaimed.

Suddenly there was the sound of a horse's pounding hoofs and several pistol shots. Freddie jumped up, his eyes wide with excitement.

"Bandits!" he shouted, racing to the driveway.

The commotion brought Mr. and Mrs. Bobbsey and the foreman running from the ranch house. As they stood and stared, a horseman galloped up the roadway.

He was a big man astride a handsome black thoroughbred. The stranger rode up to Freddie. He stretched out a long arm and scooped up the little boy. He put him on the saddle in front of him and galloped off.

He put Freddie on the saddle in front of him and galloped off

"Tom!" Mrs. Bobbsey screamed. "Where's he taking Freddie?"

The foreman laughed heartily. "Don't worry," he said. "That's Buck Tyson—owns the ranch next to us. He's a real Wild Westerner!"

In another minute the rancher rode back and lowered a beaming Freddie to the ground. Tom introduced Buck to the Bobbseys.

"We're havin' a Frontier Days barbecue over at my ranch tomorrow," the big man drawled. "We'd like you all to come wearin' old-time costumes."

"Goody!" Flossie cried, jumping up and down. "A dress-up party!" Buck Tyson waved good-by and galloped off down the lane.

A few minutes later Wes and the older twins rode in, Cinder trailing behind them. Bert described their visit to the cabin.

"We don't think Bill Dayton was there last night. I guess Cinder was lonely. We couldn't keep him from following us."

Sing Foo took the dog to the kitchen to give him some food while Mrs. Bobbsey told the three newcomers of the invitation to the barbecue.

"It sounds like fun," Nan said. "Right after dinner we must try to find some costumes."

When the meal was over, Sing Foo motioned to Mrs. Bobbsey to come into the kitchen. She returned to the living room with a broad smile on her face.

"Sing Foo is a jewel," she remarked. "He has a lot of things we can use for costumes."

The cook set up a sewing machine in the

dining room. Then he brought in a pile of flour sacks which he had saved. They were made of brightly printed material and had been washed.

"One sack will be large enough for Flossie," Mrs. Bobbsey said with a smile. "I'll sew two together for Nan and I'll need three!"

She slit the bottoms and cut armholes in the sides. They made very pretty dresses and the girls giggled as they pranced around in their flour sack dresses.

"What are Daddy and the boys going to wear?" Flossie asked.

"Sing Foo can take care of them, too. He has some black trousers which we can cut down for Bert and Freddie, and Daddy will wear an old suit that Tom's grandfather had when he was a young man."

Mrs. Bobbsey fixed the trousers for the boys, who had decided to wear plain white shirts. With their own boots and big hats they were like miniature frontiersmen.

"We don't look right!" Freddie said after he had examined himself in the mirror. "I saw some pictures of those men in a book and they all had beards!"

"Okay, we'll have beards," Bert agreed. "What will we use to make them?"

That proved to be a problem. The boys looked around the house for beard material but

could find none. Even Sing Foo could not think
of anything to use.

"Guess we'll have to forget the beards," said
Bert.

He and Freddie went out to the corral, where
Johnny Bat was practicing roping.

Freddie grabbed Bert's arm. "Maybe we
could make our beards out of rope," he proposed.

Johnny walked over to the boys, still twirling
his lariat. They told him what they wanted to
do. "Have you any old rope we can use?" Bert
asked.

The cowboy considered the matter, then said,
"I have a better idea! Come with me."

The boys followed Johnny into the old barn.
Johnny walked over to a bin against one wall.
He reached in and pulled out a pair of fur
leggings.

"What's that?" Freddie asked, reaching over
and touching the soft fur.

"These are angora-hair chaps," Johnny told
him. "We wear them in bad weather because
they're warm and shed the rain. These were left
here a couple of years ago by a cowboy who
went to the Southwest. They're too old and worn
to be much use to anyone. I'm sure it'll be okay
to cut off the fur for your beards."

"Boy!" Bert cried. "This will be neat!
Thanks, Johnny!"

Happily the boys carried their find into the dining room where their mother and sisters were still working on the costumes. Nan and Flossie helped them cut off the hair and paste it on strips of dark cloth.

"How will we keep the beards on?" Bert asked as he held one up to admire it.

Mrs. Bobbsey took the strip of cloth and sewed a string loop at each end. "Just put the loops over your ears," she instructed.

Bert and Freddie did this. When they moved their chins, the beards waggled up and down.

The girls burst into giggles and Flossie said, "You don't 'zactly look bee-yoo-ti-ful!"

At that moment Wes came into the room. "The sheriff just called," the boy reported excitedly. "He has found out what happened to Bill Dayton!"

"What?" the twins asked eagerly.

Wes said the sheriff had seen Bill in Vinton that morning. The cowboy had been riding past the Half Circle south range when he had spotted some strange cowhands driving cattle out through a break in the fence.

"What did Bill do?" Bert asked.

"He followed them, but his horse slipped off the edge of a gully and slid down to the bottom. Bill was thrown against a rock and dazed. When he came to, his horse wasn't in sight."

"What happened next?" Nan urged Wes on.

"Bill couldn't find his horse, but he managed to reach a road and was picked up by a man from Vinton." Wes went on to say that Bill had stayed overnight with the man and had been trying to buy another horse when the sheriff met him.

"Sheriff Werner told him we'd returned his horse, so he has gone back to his cabin."

"Now we can talk to Bill!" Nan said hopefully. "Let's go soon!"

"Yes," Bert agreed. "And we must return his dog. Come on, Cinder!" he called. "It's time for us to go to bed."

The big dog had adopted Bert and had followed him around all day. He settled down on the floor of the boy's first-floor bedroom.

In the middle of the night Bert was awakened by a whimper from Cinder. The boy sat up in bed just in time to see the dog jump up and run to the open window.

The next moment Cinder leaped over the sill into the darkness!

CHAPTER XIV

THE SINGING BARBECUE

IN a moment Bert recovered from his surprise.
He dashed to the window and peered into the
starry night. In the distance he saw a rider
galloping toward the ranch gate. Cinder raced
at the horse's heels.

"I wonder who that man is," Bert mused,
"and whether Cinder is chasing or just following him." The boy waited at the window for a
while, but neither the dog nor the horseman
returned. Finally Bert went back to bed, his
thoughts in a whirl.

"Maybe the man is someone Cinder recognized," he guessed. "Bill Dayton?"

The next morning when the twins went out to
the corral, Johnny Bat greeted them. "Got my
good rope back last night! Now I can show you
some real ropin'."

"Where did you find it?" Nan asked.

"Right where it's s'posed to be—on a hook in

the bunkhouse," the cowboy replied, "but the rope Bill Dayton left is gone!"

"Now I'm sure I saw Bill!" Bert disclosed. He told about Cinder jumping from the window and following the horseman.

Johnny took off his big hat and scratched his head. "Could have been Bill," he agreed, "but I can't figure why he'd sneak in here at night without tellin' anybody."

Sing Foo had come out to the corral and stood listening to the conversation. He shook his head and muttered, "Very strange doings! Rope go away, rope come back!" Still talking to himself, he shuffled off toward the kitchen.

Presently it was time to get ready for Buck Tyson's barbecue. Mr. and Mrs. Bobbsey and the twins had a good time putting on their outfits. Mrs. Bobbsey and the girls looked pretty in their bright prints. When they were dressed, and Freddie and Bert had looped on their fur beards, Wes took the family's picture with Nan's camera.

Tom Yager brought around the station wagon and they got in. At the last minute Flossie was missing.

"Where is she?" Mrs. Bobbsey looked worried.

"Here I am!" Flossie called, running from the house with her doll in her arms. "I went back for Linda!"

Flossie held up the doll, which was dressed in a little hoop-skirted costume. "Linda has on an old-fashioned costume, and she hasn't ever been to a barbecue!"

Freddie grinned. "Too bad she can't eat."

It was a twenty-minute drive to the Tyson ranch. When Tom turned into the grounds, the visitors saw that there were already a large number of people wandering around outside.

The low, rambling house was set in a grove of trees. Tables had been put up, and the guests were bustling to and fro. All wore Frontier Days costumes—the women in long skirts and sunbonnets and the men in dark suits and wide-brimmed hats.

"Welcome, folks!" Buck Tyson called.

The husky ranch owner was clad in a white fringed buckskin suit and carried a large white sombrero. He introduced the Bobbseys to his other guests, then took the twins over to see the barbecue pit.

It was about six feet long and three feet deep. Mr. Tyson explained that a fire had been built in the pit the day before. That morning chunks of seasoned meat had been wrapped in foil and sacking and placed in the pit on the hot coals.

"Finally we cover the whole thing with sand," their host said. "We're just about to take the meat out now." He signaled to two cowboys.

Under his direction they cleared away the sand from the top of the pit and lifted out the bundles with shovels. They then carried the steaming packages of meat over to one of the tables.

Flossie had been very interested in the barbecue pit. When the others went over to the table, the little girl stayed behind. She leaned over the edge of the pit to get a better view of the coals. Suddenly the doll dropped from her grasp!

"Oh!" Flossie screamed. "Linda will be burned up! Somebody save her!"

Quickly Nan ran back. She grabbed a long iron fork which had been left near the pit. Throwing herself on the ground, she reached into the trench with the fork.

"Hurry! Hurry!" Flossie begged. "My dolly will burn up!"

Nan managed to catch one of the prongs in Linda's dress and pulled up the doll. Its clothing was only slightly scorched.

"Oh, thank you, Nan!" Flossie cried, hugging Linda in her arms.

"Come to the table, little ladies!" Buck Tyson called out.

"Ooh, doesn't everything look scrumptious!" Flossie exclaimed when she saw the array of food.

The meat had been sliced into juicy pieces. There were bowls of barbecue sauce made of

"Hurry, Nan!" Flossie begged. "My dolly will burn up!"

peppers, tomatoes and onions. The table also held big dishes of creamy coleslaw, casseroles of baked beans and platters of sliced red tomatoes. Baskets of hot rolls stood nearby, covered with white napkins. Several women walked around, serving hot and cold drinks. There was plenty of laughter and everyone was very friendly to the Bobbseys.

"I like barbecues," said Freddie. "When I grow up I'm going to run our ranch and have barbecues and rodeos and—"

Flossie giggled. "And not be a fireman?" she teased.

After the dessert of strawberry shortcake had been eaten, the tables were cleared.

"What happens now?" Bert asked the boy seated next to him.

"Some of the cowboys on Buck's ranch are good singers," the boy replied. "They usually put on a terrific show when we have a barbecue."

Most of the children seated themselves on the grass. The women took places on benches or folding chairs while the men lounged on the ground or against the trees.

When they were settled, two cowboys sauntered out in front of the group. One was tall with dark hair, the other shorter and had red hair. They began strumming guitars and singing.

The audience applauded. "Yea, Red! Yea, Dude!" they cried.

The cowboy called Red pulled up a chair and sat down. The tall one, Dude, stretched out on the ground at his feet. The two strummed a few chords, then Red broke into a slow song.

"Out in the mesquite and sagebrush
  Things haven't changed since the gold rush.
  The cowhand still rises
  While the range is asleep,
  Doesn't get prizes
  From the men who tend sheep.
  His old pinto pony is still his best friend;
  His goal is the chuckhouse at the day's end."

Everyone clapped and many grinned, but Nan said, "That's a nice song, but sort of sad."

Cowboy Dude heard her and sat up. "Here's a funny one for you," he said with a smile.

"Sittin' 'neath the twinkling stars
  Strummin' my guitar
  I saw a little dogie
  A-wanderin' too far."

He winked at Nan and went on:

"I jumped up on my bronc
  An' urged the critter back.
  He bawled and ran to his old cow's side.
  She up and give him a smack!
  Yippee-i, Yippee-a!"

At a signal from the singer, the onlookers sang the last line once more, ending with *Yip-pee-i, Yippee-a!*

"That's fun!" Freddie cried. "Let's do it again."

So, with Dude teaching them one line at a time, the audience learned the song about the little lost calf. Then both cowboys entertained with several other songs, and the children joined in the choruses. They were doing a particularly lively one when Wes suddenly pointed across to a field.

"A brush fire!" he cried.

Everyone looked up. Dry grass in the far field was ablaze. The fire was spreading rapidly toward the ranch house!

CHAPTER XV

COW IN A BOG

"FIRE!" Buck Tyson shouted.

All the people at the barbecue jumped up. Many of the cowboys and the men guests dashed toward the house. In seconds they were back, carrying brooms, old saddle slickers, feed sacks, and saddle blankets. Other cowboys ran for buckets of water. The men wet the sacks and blankets and ran with them toward the approaching blaze.

"Can't we help?" Bert asked Buck Tyson.

"You and the other youngsters fill the buckets from the well. We'll try to beat the fire out, but we should have water handy in case we need it."

"I want to help!" Freddie cried, his cheeks red with excitement. He started to run across the lawn toward the burning field.

"Freddie! Come back!" his mother called. "The best way you can help is to fill the water buckets."

Reluctantly, Freddie returned to join the other children at the well. They could see the flames clearly now. The fire was moving rapidly toward the ranch house.

"Here comes Mr. Dawkins!" Bert shouted as a jeep sped up the lane.

The car came to a stop and six men jumped out. "Kirby saw the fire and sent us volunteers here," Dawkins explained.

Buck Tyson rushed up. "Glad to see you," he cried. "The fire's gaining on us. What do you think we should do?"

Dawkins peered at the advancing smoke. "We'll backfire," he declared.

With a piercing whistle, he called in the cowboys and ranchers who were out fighting the blaze. When they were back at the edge of the field, one of the fire fighters ran along the border with a flaming sack and ignited the grass.

"Why is he doing that?" Nan asked in astonishment. "I thought we were trying to put out the fire!"

Wes explained that backfiring was often used to check an approaching blaze. "We burn over a strip of ground, and when the fire gets to that place, it dies out because there is nothing more to burn."

The guests and cowboys had lined up along the edge of the field. When the blaze set by the volunteers had burned a strip of thirty feet, they ran in and extinguished it.

"Oh, I hope the backfiring works," Bert thought anxiously.

The crowd watched in tense silence as the brush fire reached the burned-over area. Finding nothing to feed on, it gradually died out.

"Yippee!" A cheer went up from the onlookers.

There was much buzzing about what or who had started the fire. No one had a clue, but Flossie whispered to Nan, "Maybe the rustlers did it!"

"Perhaps," Nan answered thoughtfully.

After such an exciting day it was difficult for the twins to go to sleep that night. Bert was still awake when he heard the owl hoot again.

"I'll bet that's a signal," he told himself.

He got up quietly, put on a robe and slippers, and went outside. To his surprise he met his father. "You heard a noise?" Mr. Bobbsey whispered.

His son nodded and the two headed for the corral. Just as they reached it, Del Logan rode out and galloped down the lane.

"Now where is *he* going?" Bert asked suspiciously.

"Probably on legitimate business," his father replied.

The next morning Bert hurried back to the corral. Del was not there, and the cowboys did not know where he had gone.

When the other children came out, Bert suggested riding to the south range to see if any more cattle were missing.

"Dad says we have to leave next Tuesday," he pointed out, "and we haven't solved the mystery yet!"

Wes was willing to go with the Bobbseys so they saddled the horses and the two ponies and set off for the grazing area. As the riders neared the fenced-in section, they heard a loud *mooo, mooo*.

Nan listened intently. "Some cow's in trouble!"

Wes urged his horse into a canter. "She must be bogged down!"

Hurrying after Wes, the other children saw the cow floundering desperately in the mud of a water hole, trying to lift her feet out. She had evidently been crowded at the edge and had fallen in.

"Maybe we can pull her out," Wes spoke up. He took his rope from the saddle horn. Twirling it, he tossed the loop over the cow's horns. The horse backed up, but the cow did not budge!

"Have to get her legs loose from the mud," Wes said, dismounting.

Bert slid from his saddle to help. The two boys waded into the water hole and finally succeeded in yanking the cow's legs free. Wes jumped quickly onto his horse again. This time he was able to pull the animal out on her back. Mooing loudly, she lay weak and helpless.

"Now's the tricky part, Bert," said Wes. "She may get ornery. Bossy here is probably mad. Once we turn her over, you run out of the way in case she charges us!"

Bert grasped the cow's horns while the ranch boy held her tail. At a signal from Wes, they flipped the animal onto her feet.

"Now let go the horns, Bert," said Wes. "We'll hop on our horses pronto!"

Bert followed instructions and quickly mounted. Wes dropped the cow's tail. Unfortunately, Wes's horse had backed farther away, and the boy had more distance to cover than he had expected.

The angry cow wheeled about and charged. Wes leaped into the saddle, but the tip of the animal's horn ripped a long tear in his jeans. All the young riders retreated to a safe distance.

"Are you hurt, Wes?" Nan asked anxiously.

"Just a scratch," he assured her.

"Why did the cow want to hurt you when you pulled her out of the mud?" asked Flossie.

Wes grinned. "Because sometimes a cow can be a plain ornery critter," he replied.

Wes pulled the cow out on her back

By this time she had mingled with the rest of the herd and was grazing peacefully.

"Do you think more cattle have been stolen?" Freddie wanted to know.

"I really can't tell for sure," Wes replied. "Let's check the fence for any signs that it has been cut."

Although the children rode around the entire grazing area, they saw nothing suspicious. Finally they turned back home.

"I know a good place to eat our lunch," Wes said. "Near a cool stream where we can have a drink of water."

"Goody!" Flossie said. "I'm getting hungry. And Sing Foo gave me a s'prise for you all!"

When they reached the end of the Half Circle

property, Freddie begged, "Let me open the gate!"

The others reined in and waited while he slid from his saddle and ran to the swinging gate. Just as he reached it, Freddie stooped and picked up something from the ground.

"What's this, Wes?" he asked and carried the object to him.

The ranch boy looked at it carefully. "This is a hatband," he said, "and a good one."

The band was of woven horsehair in shades of tan and brown. It was fastened at the side with a round silver ornament.

"Say!" Bert exclaimed. "That looks like one I saw Del Logan wearing on his hat the other day!"

"Okay, Freddie, you can give it back to Del." Wes handed the hatband to Freddie, who carefully put it in his saddlebag.

A little while later the young riders reached the picnic place. They carefully tied their horses to the trees and soon settled down near the bank of the stream to eat their sandwiches.

"Come on, Flossie," said Freddie a little later, "Where's Sing Foo's surprise?"

Flossie ran back to her pony and took a package from the saddlebag. "Special Chinese cookies!" she said. "They have fortunes inside! Sing Foo ordered them from the store just for us!"

She passed the crisp little pastries around to each one. Freddie opened his first and drew out a tiny printed slip.

"What does it say?" Flossie demanded.

Slowly Freddie spelled out the words: *"Never play with fire."* When the others laughed, he said solemnly, "The fortuneteller knows I'm going to be a fireman when I grow up."

"What's your fortune, Flossie?" Wes asked.

Flossie giggled as she read: " *'Your blue eyes will carry you far!'* "

Bert's fortune was *"There's a dark man in your future!"*

When Wes saw his, he blushed to the roots of his blond hair. It said: *"A dark-eyed girl has designs on you!"*

"What's yours, Nan?" Flossie cried, jumping up and running over to her sister.

"Mine says, *'Those near to you are acting mysteriously.'* "

"Your fortune is the best, Nan," Bert said. "I wish it could tell us where to find the mysterious rustlers before we go home."

The picnickers enjoyed a cool drink from the swift running stream and then mounted their horses. When the twins and Wes reached the ranch late in the afternoon, they unsaddled their horses at once. Then Freddie ran to look for Del Logan. He was not in the corral.

"I think he's over at the bunkhouse," Johnny said.

While the others walked up to the ranch house, Bert and Freddie went to the cowboys' quarters. Del was lounging in front.

"I found your hatband," Freddie cried, running up to the surly-looking man.

Del looked startled but reached out to take the band. "I—I rode out early to check on the cattle," he said. "I must have lost it then."

Bert decided to say nothing about having seen the cowboy leave during the night. But he felt fairly sure now that Del Logan was involved with the cattle rustlers who worked at night. What should he do about it?

CHAPTER XVI

HORSEBACK DETECTIVES

DEL Logan was not friendly with the other cowboys, Bert had noticed, and he seemed to resent the children. The boy decided to watch Del more closely.

The next morning Mr. and Mrs. Bobbsey set off with Tom Yager on horseback to make another tour of the ranch. The older twins went out to the corral to talk to Johnny Bat. Wes had gone to town on an errand for his father.

"How are you young detectives gettin' along?" Johnny asked, looking up from a saddle he was mending.

"We're not doing very well," Nan admitted. "We haven't been able to find the cattle rustlers, and we haven't found out anything about Bud Hixon, except that he comes to the Indian Reservation once in a while."

Bert said it was important that the Bobbseys talk to Bill Dayton.

Nan spoke up. "We thought that since he came here from the East he might know something about Bud."

"That's a mighty interestin' story," Johnny remarked. "Bill's a nice boy. He'll be glad to help you if he can."

"But we have such a hard time finding him!" Nan wailed.

"He'll ride in here some day," Johnny assured her. Then he had a sudden thought. "There's another cowboy out here who came from the East. Maybe he could help you!"

"There is?"

"Who is he?"

"Dude—over at Buck Tyson's ranch—came here about ten years ago. They say he's from the East."

"Do you know from what part?" Nan asked in excitement.

Johnny shook his head. "Nope. He never said, and out here we don't ask that kind of question. He might have been in some sort of trouble and come West to forget it."

"Nan!" Bert cried, "let's ride over to Tyson's and talk to Dude."

"All right," Nan agreed. "He looked friendly the other day when he was singing and playing the guitar. I'm sure he wouldn't mind talking to us."

"Maybe Dude is Bud!" Bert suggested.

"Does Dude have a crooked little finger on his right hand?" Nan asked Johnny.

The cowboy admitted he had never noticed.

"Come to think of it," he said, "Dude most always wears gloves when he's workin'."

"We'll find out!" Nan promised.

She ran into the house to tell Freddie and Flossie where they were going while Bert saddled the horses. Nan found the younger twins looking excited.

"Guess who's coming here!" Flossie cried. "Rainbow and River Deer!"

Hearing this, Nan was sorry to be leaving. But she thought her errand important. A few minutes after she and Bert had mounted their horses and set off for the Tyson ranch, the Indian children rode in on pinto ponies. They said they could not stay long but had a message for the twins.

"Man you try find—he come to Indian village," River Deer said.

"One sun ago," Rainbow added, and the Bobbseys knew she meant the day before.

Freddie asked eagerly, "Did you tell him we want to see him?"

The Indians bobbed their heads. "No good," said River Deer. "He says no want to come here."

"Why not?" Flossie asked. The children shrugged.

In a few minutes Rainbow said they must leave. The twins thanked them for bringing the message, and waved good-by.

"I wonder why Bud Hixon won't visit us," Flossie mused.

At this moment Freddie's attention was drawn to the corral. Del Logan, riding a new horse, was making the animal turn from one side to the other.

"Let's watch," Freddie said. When he and Flossie reached the fence, he asked Johnny what Del was doing.

"He's bronc bustin'," Johnny explained. "Breakin' in a wild horse."

"Will you get our ponies ready, Johnny?" Flossie pleaded. "Bert and Nan have gone off and we want to ride."

"Sure!" The good-natured Indian saddled the ponies and helped the twins mount. Then he went off to the stables to do some chores.

"Where shall we ride?" Flossie asked.

"Let's shadow Del. I 'spect him," said Freddie. "He acted awful funny when I gave him back his hatband."

Flossie's blue eyes brightened. "Maybe we can solve the mystery while Bert and Nan are away!"

The twins rode around slowly, keeping watch on the cowboy. Finally Del dismounted and took the saddle off the bronc.

"What's he going to do now?" Flossie asked.
"Watch!"

The cowboy tossed the saddle onto the back of another horse and fastened the girth. The next moment he mounted, rode out of the corral and down the lane.

"He's going away! What'll we do now?" cried Flossie.

"Follow him," Freddie insisted.

"Oh, but we're not s'posed to ride out alone," Flossie objected.

"We won't be alone," Freddie argued. "We'll be with Del. If we're going to be detectives, we'll have to find out where he's going!"

Reluctantly, Flossie agreed. The small twins turned their ponies into the lane and rode after the cowboy.

In the meantime, Bert and Nan had reached the Tyson ranch. The owner saw them coming and hurried to greet them. "Have you come back for more barbecue?" he boomed.

Bert laughed. "It was very good, sir, but my sister and I rode over here to speak to your cowboy named Dude, if we may."

"Dude? Sure! I just saw him go down to the bunkhouse. It's over there beyond those trees."

Bert and Nan headed for the bunkhouse. When they reached the low building, several cowboys were coming out.

"Is Dude here?" Bert asked one of them.

"Dude!" the cowboy called. "You got visitors!"

The tall, lanky rancher came to the door. "Hi, Nan! Hi, Bert!" he said. "You want to see me?"

Nan thought excitedly, "He's tall and he has dark, curly hair! He *could* be Bud Hixon!"

"We hear you came from the East," Bert began when the other cowboys had left. "May we ask you some questions?"

Dude's expression became guarded. "Well, I don't know," he remarked. "I've forgotten all about the East. I'd rather not talk about it."

"But if someone wanted you to come back, wouldn't you like to know?" Nan asked kindly.

"There isn't anybody'd want me to come back," Dude replied. "I don't know what you mean."

"Did you ever live in Lakeport?" Bert spoke up quickly.

Dude shook his head.

"Did you ever know anyone who came from there?" Nan persisted. "Someone named Bud Hixon?"

Again Dude shook his head. Desperately, Nan looked at the cowboy's hands. He was wearing gloves. She *must* find out about his little finger. Nan put a hand into the pocket of her jeans and pulled out a chocolate bar which she had saved from her lunch the day before.

"Would you like some candy?" She held the package out to Dude.

"Thanks." He took it and tried to slide off the wrapper. But the gloves made him clumsy. Quickly he pulled off the right glove and unwrapped the candy.

Nan leaned forward to look at his little finger. It was perfectly straight! He was not Bud Hixon!

Bert, also, had seen the finger. "Thanks anyway, Dude," he said, starting off.

"We didn't learn anything from him," Nan observed in a discouraged tone as they rode back toward the Half Circle.

Meanwhile, Freddie and Flossie had kept some distance behind Del Logan as he rode across the valley. But when they reached the mountains they speeded up to keep the cowboy in sight.

Freddie was so intent on trailing Del that he forgot to watch for gopher holes. Suddenly his pony stepped into one and lurched forward!

Caught by surprise, Freddie lost his balance and slid from the pony's back. Flossie quickly leaned over and caught the reins before the pony could get away.

"Are you hurt?" she asked her twin.

Sheepishly, Freddie shook his head. "But I hope my pony's all right," he said.

The animal seemed to be and Freddie climbed back into the saddle. The twins looked around for Del. He had disappeared!

"Hurry!" Freddie urged. "We mustn't lose him!"

They urged their ponies into a fast walk up the steep, rocky hillside. The path led around a huge boulder.

When they turned the corner, there was Del seated quietly on his horse, waiting for them!

"Oh!" Flossie cried, startled.

"Why are you kids followin' me?" Del asked, furious.

"We wanted to see where you were going!" Freddie spoke up bravely.

"It's none of your business where I'm goin'!" Del stormed. "Now beat it back to the ranch!"

Freddie and Flossie were frightened. They turned their ponies and retraced their path.

Mr. and Mrs. Bobbsey and Tom reached the ranch just as Bert and Nan were unsaddling their horses. They all walked into the house together.

"Where are Freddie and Flossie?" Mrs. Bobbsey asked Sing Foo.

The Chinese cook said the last time he had seen the small twins they were riding around behind the corral.

Mrs. Bobbsey hurried outside. In a few minutes she returned. "No one has seen Freddie

Caught by surprise, Freddie lost his balance

and Flossie for two hours, Tom!" she cried.
"I'm afraid they've gone off somewhere on
their ponies."

"I'll send some of the boys to look for them,"
the foreman assured her. "Don't worry!"

But before the men could leave, Freddie and
Flossie rode in. They were surprised that a
search was about to be made for them.

"We were being detectives and following Del!" Freddie explained.

"But he got awful mad and told us to come home!" Flossie added.

"You must realize, Freddie and Flossie," Mr. Bobbsey said sternly, "that this is very big country and you could easily get lost. You must *not* leave the ranch again—even to be detectives—unless someone is with you!"

Tearfully, the small twins promised.

The four children were playing outside after dinner when Dawkins drove up to the house in his jeep. The twins ran to greet him.

"Have you found your calf Star?" he asked Freddie.

"No," Freddie replied, looking sad. "He was stolen again."

"Well, I've just been up to see Kirby," Dawkins continued, "and she thinks she saw Star near Red Canyon Gap!"

CHAPTER XVII

A TRUCK PRISONER

"KIRBY saw Star!" Freddie cried. "Come on! We have to get her back!"

"Hold on, Freddie!" Bert said. "We don't even know where Red Canyon Gap is!"

"Ask Tom Yager," Dawkins advised. "I have to get along, but I wanted you to know about Star."

"Thank you very much, Mr. Dawkins," Freddie said.

When Tom joined the Bobbseys at the supper table the twins told him what Dawkins had reported and asked about Red Canyon Gap.

"That was a famous hideout for bandits in the days of the Old West," the foreman explained. "There's only one entrance to the canyon. Outlaws used to hole up inside and nobody could get them out."

"Wow!" said Bert. "I'd like to see it."

"And I have to rescue Star!" Freddie cried.

"Don't count on finding Star there," Tom remarked. "But if you'd all like to see the gap, it would make a good overnight camping trip. Wes could take you."

"Oh, yes!" Flossie exclaimed. "We haven't been camping for a long while! I want to sleep outdoors."

Mr. and Mrs. Bobbsey agreed that the trip would be fun. It was decided that they would start out the next afternoon for Red Canyon.

In the morning the Bobbseys drove into Vinton to church. Then, after one of Sing Foo's delicious dinners, preparations for the camping trip began.

"We have sleeping bags enough for Mr. and Mrs. Bobbsey and two of the children," Tom Yager reported.

"Wes and the other twins will have to take roundup beds."

"What are roundup beds?" Bert inquired.

"They're the kind of beds the cowboys take out on roundup work," Wes replied. "We make them ourselves."

"I want a roundup bed!" Freddie decided.

"Okay," Wes agreed. "We'll make them up for you and Bert. The girls can use the sleeping bags."

While the others watched with interest, Wes assembled the beds. First, he spread out a large tarpaulin—a piece of waterproof canvas—on the floor. In the center of this he put two quilts for a mattress, then a pair of cotton blankets.

"We sleep between these," he explained.

Next came two woolen blankets. Then the tarpaulin was folded over the quilts and blankets, fastened with snaps, and rolled up.

Bert and Freddie helped make up their beds and carry them out to the corral. Johnny and Wes packed them on the back of a horse.

"We're taking two pack horses," Wes told them, "one to carry the bedrolls and one for the food supplies."

It was late afternoon by the time the camping party was ready to set out. Sing Foo, Tom Yager, and several cowboys gathered to wave good-by.

Wes was first in line, leading one of the pack horses. The Bobbseys followed, with Bert at the rear leading the other pack horse.

They rode across the valley at an easy pace for a half hour. Then Wes halted his horse and dismounted.

"I want to check the packs," he explained. "Sometimes after they've settled a bit, they get loose." He quickly took up the slack in the lash ropes, and the riders went on.

It was almost dark by the time they reached a point in the mountains where Wes stopped,

this time in a wooded spot. Ahead, the Bobbseys could see a rocky wall cut by a deep gash
through which flowed a river.

"This is the entrance to Red Canyon Gap,"
Wes said. "We can camp here by the river in
this grove."

"It's perfect!" the twins' mother exclaimed.

Mr. Bobbsey and Bert set to work unpacking
the beds and supplies. Wes built a fire among
some rocks on the riverbank.

Then, while Mr. Bobbsey and the boys fed,
watered, and tied up the horses for the night,
Nan and Flossie helped their mother prepare
supper.

Soon slices of ham and potatoes were sizzling
in the frying pan. There was a Thermos of hot
cocoa for the children and coffee for the grownups. Sing Foo had baked a special apple pie
for dessert.

"Ooh!" Flossie exclaimed as she finished her
piece. "It tasted scrumptious, just like Dinah's
pie."

As they sat around the campfire, the children and Wes began singing cowboy songs. Before long, Flossie's head began to nod.

"Sleep time," said Mrs. Bobbsey. A little
while later, Nan, Flossie, and their parents were
snugly tucked into sleeping bags.

Wes showed the boys how to fasten the tarpaulin at the sides of the roundup beds so the

wind could not come through. Soon they too were fast asleep.

During the night Bert was awakened by a rumbling sound. "It must be the river," he told himself. Then, fully awake, he realized it was not the river.

He sat up and peered into the darkness. He could make out the dim shapes of two trucks lumbering up the narrow mountain road.

"What would trucks be doing here?" Bert wondered. "Something to do with the rustlers?"

He looked over at Wes. The boy's head was covered by the tarpaulin, and he was sleeping soundly. "I'm probably wrong," Bert decided.

No one else had awakened, and finally Bert settled down in his bed again.

The next thing he knew it was daylight and the delicious odor of frying bacon came to him. Bert jumped up and made his way to the river-bank where Wes and Nan were washing their faces.

When Bert told them about the trucks he had seen during the night, Wes was amazed. "This road doesn't lead any place," he said. "There's no outlet at the end of the canyon. The trucks will have to come back this way. Maybe we can find out more then."

After a hearty breakfast of fruit juice, bacon, and pancakes, Nan and Flossie helped their mother wash the utensils in the river.

Bert told his parents about the trucks. "Wes and Nan and I want to explore the canyon and see where they went."

"Run along," Mr. Bobbsey agreed. "Freddie and Flossie and I are going to do some fishing."

"Don't forget to look for Star," Freddie said.

When Wes and the older twins reached the road, Bert pointed to heavy tire marks in the dust. "Here they are! I wasn't dreaming!"

The children followed the tracks for some time. Then, as the trio rounded a corner, they came upon four big trucks parked where the road ended.

"This is the mouth of the canyon and the only entrance," Wes whispered to the twins.

Cautiously they moved toward the vehicles. No one was around. Evidently the drivers had gone farther into the canyon on foot.

"It's sure queer!" Wes observed. "I wonder what's doing."

The three children walked closer to examine the trucks. As they did, Nan stopped suddenly. "Listen!" she whispered. "Something's moving in the back of that truck!" She pointed to the last one in line.

Thump, thump, thump. Nan went nearer. "Is someone inside?" she called.

A low whine answered. "Open the door, Bert," she urged.

There was only a simple catch on the rear

door, and Bert quickly unlatched it. On the floor of the otherwise empty interior lay a cowboy and a dog! Both were tied and gagged.

Bert and Wes jumped into the truck and bent to untie the prisoners. As Wes peered at the man he exclaimed in astonishment:

"Bill Dayton!"

"And Cinder!" Nan cried. She pulled the gag from around the dog's muzzle, and he immediately licked her cheek. When his legs had been untied, he jumped and frolicked around the truck.

"Down, Cinder!" Bill called. The dog sat, still wagging his tail furiously.

The cords binding Bill proved to be difficult to loosen. Nan climbed into the truck to help the boys. "Let me try!" she said and bent over the knots. Then suddenly she straightened.

Bert stared as his twin pointed to Bill's little finger. It was crooked!

"Are you the missing Bud Hixon?" Nan asked.

For a second the young man looked defiantly at the youngsters. Then he said, "Yes, I am."

"Why have you been running away from us?" Bert asked.

As the children struggled to untie him, Bill said, "When I heard Tom Yager say the Bobbsey family from Lakeport was coming to the Half Circle I decided to leave. I was afraid

Nan pointed to Bill's little finger. It was crooked!

that if your parents were acquainted with my father, they might recognize me and start trouble. I want to remain Bill Dayton."

"The Indians know you by your right name," Bert put in.

"Yes," the young man admitted. "By accident I told them, but I was sure they would have no reason for mentioning me to anyone else. How did you find this out?"

Freddie answered. "We asked them!"

"Bud," Nan put in eagerly, "your father isn't angry any more and he misses you very much. He's all alone and he wants you to come back and help him at his riding stables!"

Bill thought this over a few seconds. "I'll see," he said. "But right now we're in great danger. We must get out of here!"

His cords were finally loosened.

"Quick! Tell us how you got tied up here, Bill," Wes urged.

The cowboy explained that on Saturday he and Cinder had been out tramping when they had come upon Boots Harris and his gang driving some of the Half Circle cattle out of the south range.

"Boots!" Bert exclaimed. "So he *is* one of the cattle rustlers!"

Bill nodded. "Boots recognized me. So they grabbed Cinder and me, tied us up and kept us in a mountain cabin hideout until last night."

"The cabin we found!" Nan cried.

"Then they put us in this truck and drove up here."

Bert asked if Bill had seen Del Logan among his captors. The young man shook his head. "But I think there are more of the gang in hiding."

"What *is* going on in the canyon, Bill?" Wes asked.

"The rustlers have all the stolen cattle up there. They're going to herd them into the trucks and take them to the Chicago cattle market."

"We must notify the sheriff and stop them!" Wes cried.

Everyone scrambled toward the truck doors. At the same moment they heard heavy footsteps approaching!

Nan gasped. "The rustlers! Th—they're coming back!"

CHAPTER XVIII

AN EXCITING ROUNDUP

"WE can't leave now!" Nan whispered as the footsteps drew nearer.

"No, we're caught!" Wes agreed, closing the doors noiselessly.

He and the others crouched low, listening tensely. They could hear the sound of doors being opened and slammed shut.

"Someone is checking all the trucks," Bert murmured. "I hope he skips this one."

Cinder gave a little whine. Bill held the dog's mouth shut to keep him from barking.

The footsteps echoed on relentlessly and finally stopped at their truck. The next moment the doors were flung open. A big brawny man stuck his head inside.

"What—!" The cowman stopped in astonishment.

"Get 'im, Cinder!" Bill commanded.

With a leap the dog landed on the man's chest, knocking him to the ground.

"Come on!" Bert shouted.

Bill, Wes, and Nan scrambled from the truck after Bert. Cinder was standing over the man.

"Get off me!" the cattle thief fumed.

Bill Dayton chuckled. "Cinder won't let him go. He's a guard dog."

The four raced down the road. It did not take them long to reach the camp. Freddie was just removing a fish from his line.

"Look what I caught!" Freddie cried.

"We've caught some big fish, too!" Bert panted. He quickly explained the situation to his parents.

Mr. and Mrs. Bobbsey shook hands with Bill and said they were glad he had been found. Then they considered how to notify the sheriff.

"Kirby could use her radio," Flossie said.

"That's an idea!" Bert agreed. "How far is the fire tower from here, Wes?"

"It can't be too far, if Kirby spotted Star through binoculars," Wes replied. "The rustlers will probably try to load these cattle as fast as they can, but it will take some time. Let's go!"

Camp equipment was quickly packed and the horses saddled. Then the party started off. Bill rode Flossie's pony, while the little girl was lifted up in front of her father. Wes led the way along the side of the mountain.

After several turns, Nan pointed ahead and called, "There's the tower!"

The riders urged their horses on and a short time later reached the fire tower.

"Hello, up there!" Wes shouted.

The door onto the platform opened and Kirby stepped out. She leaned over the railing and called down a greeting.

"You and Bert go up, Wes," Mr. Bobbsey suggested. "You'll know where to tell the sheriff to find the rustlers."

The boys raced up the long flight of steps. Kirby was waiting for them at the top. "I have a freshly baked cake for you!" she said with a chuckle.

"Thanks, Kirby," Wes replied, "but we have to get in touch with Sheriff Werner right away!"

"The sheriff!" Kirby repeated. "Why?"

Bert told her about the rustlers in Red Gap Canyon. "We think they're going to truck the stolen cattle out," he said.

"Mercy sakes!" the fire watcher exclaimed. "I'll call right away!"

She hurried to the shortwave radio and soon contacted the sheriff. Wes described the location.

"I know just where you mean, Wes," the lawman said. "I'll bring my deputies and head off the gang at the bottom of the road."

"Can we go back, too?" Bert asked Wes.

"Sure," the other boy agreed.

"I'm sorry you can't stay for a visit," Kirby said, "but I'll give you some cake anyway."

"Thanks, Kirby." Bert took the box she offered. "We can eat it while we're riding!"

The riders turned their horses toward the canyon. When they reached the valley, there were no signs of either the sheriff or the rustlers.

"I hope the thieves didn't get away," Nan remarked in a worried tone.

"I don't think so," Bill assured her. "They couldn't have loaded all the cattle yet."

Bert mentioned a new worry. "Perhaps they'll take another route now that they know we saw the trucks."

Wes shook his head. "There's no other way the trucks can get down from the canyon. They sure can't be driven cross-country."

Just then Bill called out. "Here comes the posse!"

The others turned to see six men headed by Sheriff Werner riding at full gallop across the valley.

"Good work, Wes!" the sheriff said when his group reached the waiting party.

"If Bert Bobbsey here hadn't seen the trucks last night, we wouldn't have located the thieves," Wes explained.

"You're good detectives!" The sheriff smiled

broadly. "Now you'll have to get out of sight. I don't want anybody hurt."

Everyone hastily dismounted. Then Mr. Bobbsey and the older boys led the horses off some distance and tied them in a clump of trees. In a few moments the campers were crouched behind the huge boulders which littered the area.

Suddenly Bill felt a warm tongue touch his cheek. "Cinder!" he cried. "Good boy!"

The dog whined joyfully and wagged his plumed tail. At a word from his master, he settled down quietly.

Bert had been thinking of the mysterious figure he had seen coming from the bunkhouse on two different occasions. Now he told Bill about this. "Was it you?" he asked.

"Yes," Bill admitted. "I forgot my rope when I left. I sneaked back one night to get it and picked up Johnny's exhibition rope by mistake. The night I brought it back, Cinder heard me and followed me home."

He patted the dog affectionately. A minute later a rumbling sound was heard. It grew louder.

"The trucks!" Bert exclaimed.

He and the others peered out excitedly.

"Here they come!" Freddie yelled.

The heavy trucks could now be seen approaching. The posse tensed for action.

As the first truck came abreast of them, the sheriff stepped into the middle of the road. "Halt!" he cried.

When all four trucks had stopped, the other members of the posse rushed out and dragged the drivers from the cabs.

The Bobbseys gasped as they emerged from their hiding places. The driver of the lead truck was the flashily dressed cowboy, Boots Harris!

Two of the posse hurried to open the rear doors of the trucks. The mooing and snorting of cattle filled the air.

Freddie could wait no longer. He ran out into the middle of the road, shouting, "Is Star there?"

By this time the sheriff and his men had the rustlers lined up, handcuffs on their wrists. Del Logan was one of them!

Freddie took the whistle from his pocket and blew on it gently. At once there was a commotion in the first truck.

Bert ran over and pulled down the ramp. "Here she is, Freddie!" The brown calf with the white star on her forehead hesitated, but the next moment she trotted slowly down the ramp.

Freddie ran up and threw his arms about the calf's neck. "I'm glad we found you, Star," he cried. "Those bad men were going to take you away!"

In the meantime, the sheriff had been ques-

The calf hesitated, then trotted slowly down the ramp

tioning Boots. The cowboy admitted that with Del's help he had been stealing from the Half Circle ranch for some time. He had tried to keep the Bobbseys away from the ranch by meeting them at the train after he had sent a fake telegram to Tom Yager announcing that the family's arrival had been delayed.

"I didn't think you'd get away from that deserted house for a long time," he remarked glumly.

"Was the branding iron we found in the mountain cabin the one you used to change the Half Circle brand?" Nan asked.

"Yes," Boots said, "and I'll bet you kids found that note I tore up because first you came to the covered wagon on the rodeo grounds and saw Del. Then you showed up at the Frontier House when we were having a meeting."

"You and your gang cut our fences and then mended them after you drove out the cattle!" Wes declared hotly.

"And it was *your* belt buckle Nan found!" Flossie guessed.

Boots shrugged. "Yep," he muttered.

"Okay," the sheriff broke in. "We have enough evidence. You and your men get in those trucks. We're taking you back to the Half Circle ranch. And don't try any funny business on the way!"

There was great excitement when the strange procession arrived at the ranch. Tom Yager and Johnny Bat were amazed and delighted at the rustlers' capture and the return of the stolen cattle.

As the prisoners were led off by the sheriff, Mr. Bobbsey looked proudly at the twins. "You children helped solve the mysteries just in time!" he remarked. "We're flying home tomorrow!"

"So soon?" Freddie wailed. "I haven't had a chance to play with Star!"

"Daddy has to get back to the lumberyard," Mrs. Bobbsey reminded him. "We'll all visit this great West again."

Nan walked over to Bill and took his hand.

"Won't you come with us? she asked softly. "We promised your father we would try to bring you back to him."

Bill looked uncertain. "We—ell, I might," he said. "But what will I do with Cinder?"

Sing Foo had come outside to announce dinner and heard Bud. "I take care of him. We good friends."

As if the dog understood the conversation, he trotted over to the good-natured cook. Cinder stood up, put his paws on Sing Foo's shoulders, and licked his cheek.

Bill laughed. "I guess Cinder won't mind too much if I go. He likes everyone!"

"Except rustlers!" Wes chuckled.

Mr. Bobbsey said he would be glad to make a reservation for Bill on the same plane the family planned to take. The cowboy borrowed a horse from the ranch and rode back to his cabin to get a suitcase.

The next day Tom and Wes drove the Bobbseys and Bill to the airport where they said good-by. As the big plane circled overhead for a few moments, Flossie peered from the window.

"I see the cake lady's fire tower!" she cried.

Freddie looked over her shoulder. "And I see Star!" he declared.

Nan grinned. "I see our friends at the Indian Reservation. Good-by, Rainbow and River Deer!"

When they landed in Lakeport, Sam was there to meet them in the station wagon. And Dinah had cooked a special welcome-home dinner.

Several days later, Bill and his father came to call on the Bobbseys. Mr. Hixon wanted to thank the twins for finding his son.

"Bill likes life in the West so much," he added, "that we're going back to Vinton to live."

"That's wonderful!" said Mrs. Bobbsey. "Tom Yager would be happy to have you both work at Half Circle Ranch!"

Bert grinned and said, "And we'll be out soon to learn some trick cowboy riding!"